WITNESS
TO THIS
GENERATION

WITNESS
TO THIS
GENERATION

Creation Evangelism for the Last Days

ROGER OAKLAND

Lighthouse Trails Publishing
Eureka, Montana

Library of Congress Cataloging-in-Publication Data
Names: Oakland, Roger, 1947- author.
Title: Witness to this generation : creation evangelism for the last days /
   Roger Oakland.
Description: 2nd [edition]. | Eureka : Lighthouse Trails Publishing,
2018.
Identifiers: LCCN 2018041426 | ISBN 9781942423409 (softbound
: alk. paper)
Subjects: LCSH: Evangelistic work. | Missions. | Creationism. | End
of the world.
Classification: LCC BV3793.O34 2018 | DDC 269/.2--dc23 LC
record available at https://lccn.loc.gov/2018041426.

Note: Lighthouse Trails Publishing books are available at special quan-
tity discounts. Contact information for publisher in back of book.

Printed in the United States of America

CONTENTS

And the times of this ignorance God winked at; but now commandeth all men every where to repent: Because he hath appointed a day, in the which he will judge the world in righteousness by that man whom he hath ordained; whereof he hath given assurance unto all men, in that he hath raised him from the dead. (Acts 17: 30-31)

PROLOGUE

This book has been written for people who have a desire to share their faith in the God of the Bible with others. If you have accepted Jesus Christ as your Lord and Savior and you know someone who has not, then this book has been specifically written for you.

Several years ago, when the outline for this book first came together, I was immediately excited. Ever since becoming a follower of Jesus Christ, God gave me a strong desire to share my faith with others. And it seemed apparent that most of the Christians I knew also wanted to proclaim the "Good News" to friends, relatives, and acquaintances whom they knew were on a path headed towards a lost eternity. I thought that a book that would share biblical principles about witnessing would be well-received by the Christian community.

The title I chose for the book was *Witnessing to This Generation*. After submitting the book in outline form to three different Christian publishers, my enthusiasm was soon dampened. A book on the subject of witnessing, they said, did not fit with their publishing plans. One publisher told me their company had tried a book on the subject of witnessing before, but it had not been financially successful. Most Christians, it was stated, are not interested in the area of effective Christian witnessing.

Somewhat disappointed, I continued the outline, certain there was a need for a practical book on this subject. The more I thought and prayed about the project, the more convinced I was that I should proceed.

If the foundational principal of Christianity is recognizing who Jesus is and what He has done, I reasoned, then sharing this truth with unbelievers should be next in line. If we follow Jesus' New Testament commandment, which challenges us to love God first and then our neighbors before ourselves, should we not do everything in our power to share the Good News of God's saving grace with others?

Over the next several months as the outline was transformed into paragraphs, pages, and then chapters, it became apparent to me there was an even greater urgency to complete this book. If, as many Christians believe, we are living at the very period of history when Jesus Christ could return, should we not be doing everything possible to tell the lost how they can know Him as their Savior and Friend now and not as their Judge later? And secondly, knowing the time before His return will be characterized by great deception, should we not be sharing biblical truths with those who are deceived?

The more I worked on the book, the more uncomfortable I became about the title I had chosen. *Witnessing to This*

Generation was too passive, I thought. The word witnessing lacked urgency and gave the feeling that proclaiming the Good News was something Christians could do if they had time left over when their other work was done.

One night, while standing before the altar at my home church in Eston, Saskatchewan, Canada, I sensed God's prompting regarding the title of the book. I sensed there was an urgency that I had not experienced before: witnessing to this generation should be changed to *witness* to this generation. Thus, the inspiration for the final title for this book.

It is my prayer that as you read the following pages, God's Holy Spirit will touch you with the same sense of urgency that I've experienced. Witnessing should not be a matter of a casual choice. It should be a burning desire and responsibility that every believer should experience daily. May God give us the wisdom and the ability to be effective witnesses in the days in which we live so that many people will hear about the miraculous message of His grace that has transformed our own lives. The time left to do so may be very short.

Roger Oakland

For I am not ashamed of the gospel of Christ: for it is the power of God unto salvation to every one that believeth; to the Jew first, and also to the Greek. (Romans 1:16)

—1—

FARMER THEOLOGY

What is the Gospel? To every Christian believer, the word *Gospel* means "the Good News." And this Good News has no denominational, racial, ethnic, or national boundaries. It is a free gift anyone can receive. Unfortunately, as simple as the Gospel is, too many people try to make it complicated. Actually, the Good News is not complicated at all.

In fact, the way to eternal life is so basic a child can easily grasp it. Perhaps that is why it seems much easier to talk to a child than to an adult about God's saving grace. If adults would humble themselves by shedding their protective layers of pride, their decision to accept God's gift of eternal life would be much easier to make.

THE GIFT

While presenting a message to a group of Spanish-speaking people in Argentina, an idea for making the message of salvation clear and understandable popped into my mind.

Speaking with the help of a translator, I mentioned that I had a copy of one of my books to give away to the first person who raised a hand. As soon as the translator finished the sentence, a small boy sitting in the front row responded. His little hand was high in the air well before any others. I invited him to come toward the platform, and without hesitation, he grabbed the book then quickly returned to his chair.

"What we all just observed," I explained to the congregation, "is a demonstration of giving and receiving. The act of giving the book required action from two different people. I was the one who gave the book, and this young boy eagerly received it. The gift of eternal life is exactly the same. God is the one who gives the gift. You and I are the ones who can choose to receive the gift. In the case of the gift of salvation, there are no limits and no shortages. There will always be enough of this gift to go around; salvation is available to all those who want to receive the free gift."

I then went on to explain to the congregation that the gift of salvation comes with just one string attached. The recipients must place their faith and trust in the saving power of the Son of God, Jesus Christ. In doing so, salvation is received, and the transforming power of the Gospel begins its work. This is a life-long process of changing the life of God's newly-adopted child from the inside out.

HE WILL DO HIS PART

God is in charge. He has all things in control. And, when it comes to salvation, He will accomplish all He intends.

Using a somewhat different metaphor than the idea of a gift, the prophet Isaiah referred to salvation as a seed. His words declare God's reliability when it comes to His gift of salvation. Isaiah stated:

> For as the rain cometh down, and the snow from heaven, and returneth not thither, but watereth the earth, and maketh it bring forth and bud, that it may give seed to the sower, and bread to the eater: So shall my word be that goeth forth out of my mouth: it shall not return unto me void, but it shall accomplish that which I please, and it shall prosper in the thing whereto I sent it. (Isaiah 55:10-11)

Throughout Scripture, God often expresses His thoughts using illustrations that involve farming terminology. In this case, the moisture from the rain and the snow provide the necessary conditions for the dormant seeds to germinate. In the same way, the Holy Spirit will stimulate growth in the dormant seeds planted by the Word of God. And once the word has been planted, it will bring forth fruit in due season. What a beautiful illustration that virtually everyone can understand.

THE PARABLE OF THE SOWER

Jesus often taught in parables, and He took Isaiah's picture of the seed a bit further in the Parable of the Sower. He was speaking to people who could relate to farming or gardening, and He described to them the different things that happened when a sower went out to sow his seed.

Some seed fell by the road, and the birds devoured it. Some seed fell on rocky soil, and as soon as it grew, it withered away. Other seed fell among weeds, and when it grew up, the plant was choked out. Still, other seed fell into good ground, grew up and produced a crop that multiplied itself a hundred-fold.

When Jesus' disciples questioned the meaning of the parable, this was His response:

> Now the parable is this: The seed is the word of God. Those by the way side are they that hear; then cometh the devil, and taketh away the word out of their hearts, lest they should believe and be saved. They on the rock are they, which, when they hear, receive the word with joy; and these have no root, which for a while believe, and in time of temptation fall away. And that which fell among thorns are they, which, when they have heard, go forth, and are choked with cares and riches and pleasures of this life, and bring no fruit to perfection. But that on the good ground are they, which in an honest and good heart, having heard the word, keep it, and bring forth fruit with patience. (Luke 8:11-15)

The parable of the sower is a perfect description of the various results that may occur when we witness to our own generation. The degree of skill with which the witness plants the seed may not necessarily be related to the failure or the success of the final harvest.

THE HARD-WORKING FARMER

In the second chapter of Timothy 2, Paul points out the attributes of a strong Christian. In verse 6, he said a believer should be like a hard-working farmer, deserving to receive the first share of the crop.

I grew up on a wheat farm, and because I treasure my farming background, this illustration is very meaningful to me. It is with this in mind that I have chosen a farming illustration to capture the essence of this book. It is my hope that this illustration will help you to remember some of the basic principles that apply to Christian witnessing, as you read the following pages of this book.

In the province of Saskatchewan in Western Canada, sometimes the farmer prepares the seed bed by "summer fallowing" the land for a complete growing season before the crop is planted. In other words, the land is taken out of production and tilled so that moisture can be preserved and weeds can be controlled. In so doing, the farmer gives the land a rest and makes it suitable for planting the seed the following year.

At seeding time, usually in the latter part of April or the first part of May, the farmer begins to plant the seed. It is important to wait until the conditions are suitable. The farmer then goes out with his seeding equipment and works long hours planting the seed. After he has planted the seed, he must undertake a few other operations to ensure everything possible has been done to provide a good seed bed.

Following all the effort and preparation that has been made, basically two things can happen: the seed will germinate if there is enough moisture, or it will lie dormant in the soil if there is none. The germination of the seed is totally dependent upon conditions which are beyond the farmer's control.

That is exactly the way it is with witnessing. You and I can do everything possible to be an effective witness. But positive evangelistic results happen not as the result of *our* might and power but by God's Spirit. Yes, we must work hard; we need to be diligent and obedient; but it is God who brings the harvest.

ARE YOU A WITNESS?

Will you be a witness to our generation? This is the challenge I place before you in this book. And, what is the difference between this generation and those that have come and gone before us, you may ask? I believe that one of the most distinguishing elements in our society is the moral and spiritual erosion brought about by a belief in evolution and by a re-emergence of paganism. Since these dangerous beliefs are especially prevalent in our contemporary culture, we must arm ourselves with specific truth in order to confront their spurious teachings. I also believe that we are living in times that the Bible calls "The Last Days." This too, should make an impact on both our motivation and our message.

With these concepts in mind, I hope you will prayerfully read on. Most of all, I encourage you to gather together your storehouse of "seed," survey the land around you, and begin the business of patiently sowing precious truth, trusting that God will provide a bountiful, eternal harvest.

—2—

WITNESSING: AN ACT OF LOVE

can vividly recall the experience as if it had just occurred yesterday. And every time I think about it, I still break out into a nervous sweat. You would think I was afraid it could happen to me all over again!

It was a sub-zero night in the winter of 1959, and I was fourteen years old. We were sitting in my high school auditorium, set in the midst of the Canadian prairies. The occasion was a small-town crusade where over four hundred people had gathered to hear a high-powered evangelist from Eastern Canada share his biblical views.

I went to the meeting with my mother. Although I had been brought up to believe in God and had gone to church from the time I was a small child, this meeting was far different from any I had ever attended. Throughout the night, the man paced from one side of the auditorium platform to the other, dramatizing the vast difference between Heaven and Hell. At the end of the meeting, he made an appeal to all those in attendance to lift up their hands. He wanted to see for himself those who wanted to go to Heaven or those who had decided to spend eternity in Hell.

With "everyone's head bowed and eyes closed," I lifted my hand confidently up into the air. Of course, I did not want to go to Hell. Who did?

Then the evangelist said something which surprised me. He requested that all those who had raised their hands should stand up and walk toward him. "You must make a public stand if you are going to follow Jesus," he bellowed. "Get up out of your chairs, and walk down to the front of this auditorium, and let everyone in this room know you want to get saved."

My heart seemed to stop beating. Is he talking about me? How could I do that? There are all kinds of people here who know who I am. They'll think I'm completely crazy! These and other terrible thoughts shot through my mind, as if a tennis player were banging a ball repetitively against a wall. The evangelist made two more appeals, each time his words were more intimidating and threatening. Still, I sat glued to my chair, my feet stuck to the floor.

Finally, after what seemed like an eternity, all those who had decided to get up and go to the front were standing for prayer. Just then, a little old lady seated behind me reached forward, tapped me on the shoulder, and whispered hoarsely in my ear, "Sonny, I saw you put your hand up. God wants you to walk up to the front and get saved. You don't want to burn in Hell, do you?"

I had already been in a state of trauma. Now I was in a fit of despair. Feelings of anger and frustration gripped me. I felt like I had been tricked and manipulated. Almost as if it were a reflex action, I suddenly jumped out of my chair. I bolted to the back of the auditorium, forced open the door, and without even stopping to put on my winter overshoes, ran non-stop a mile-and-a-half home, freezing my hands and my feet in the process.

Even as I write these few lines and relive this experience, the same emotions replay in my mind. However, now, many years later, I am able to analyze this event from a completely different perspective. After running home from the evangelist's plea to publicly commit myself to follow Christ, I continued to run, not from the evangelist, but from God. I ran for another sixteen years. It was not until I was thirty years of age that I realized I had made a serious mistake.

Although the little old lady in the high school auditorium may have been wrong in the way she challenged me to make a decision to follow Christ, I discovered later in life, the basis of what she and the evangelist had to say was absolutely true. Today, I have committed my life to share the Good News of the Gospel with others. It is my hope that I am presenting the Gospel in a way that presents Jesus Christ intelligently and without intimidation.

Although I have nothing against evangelistic crusades, my personal belief is that every individual believer has been called to be an evangelist by sharing his or her faith with others, one-on-one. It is my prayer that this book will contribute in some way to help Christians who read it to plant seeds of truth that God can germinate.

THE MOST LOVING GIFT WE CAN OFFER

Jesus Christ proclaimed these following important words:

> Thou shalt love the Lord thy God with all thy heart,
> and with all thy soul, and with all thy mind. This is
> the first and great commandment. And the second
> is like unto it, Thou shalt love thy neighbour as
> thyself. On these two commandments hang all the
> law and the prophets. (Matthew 22:37-40)

For a follower of Jesus Christ, it is quite clear that the most important thing we can do, next to loving God, is to love others. Without question, telling people about Jesus is the most loving act we can perform toward them. It's really not an option, and all believers have been called to participate.

However, in this very complex world, there are many obstacles to evangelism. Satan has a clever agenda to deceive mankind and sabotage the plan of God. Preventing us from sharing God's plan of salvation is one of Satan's greatest objectives. As much as we may long to see others receive the Good News of salvation, it is not always easy to be a messenger of God's loving gift to them.

As well, many Christians are unaware that, at the very moment they made a decision to follow Jesus Christ, they immediately stepped onto the frontline of a raging battle. In fact, a new believer has walked out of the enemy camp, crossed over the frontline, and exchanged allegiances. Once lost in the kingdom of darkness, he or she instantaneously becomes a soldier of God enlisted in the most important battle in the history of the universe. How well these "new recruits" perform depends on their willingness to follow the will of God.

As one of their duties in the battle, God's soldiers are called to be witnesses for His Kingdom. In fact, this is a primary responsibility that all Christians share.

PREPARATION FOR THE WITNESS STAND

Being called as a witness in a courtroom situation can be a difficult experience. To be a good Christian witness, it is important to have a clear understanding of *what* you believe, and *why* you believe. When the judge or the jury's ultimate decision is on the line, the information presented by all the witnesses has to be weighed and evaluated. Every word that has been said is taken into consideration. In the same sense, if we are going to be witnesses for Jesus Christ, we need to be properly prepared if we are going to present an effective case. How do you know that Jesus Christ provided the only way for salvation? Are you sure about what you believe, or are you only going on emotions or feelings?

Maybe one reason you are reading this book is to help prepare yourself for the "witness stand." Is there someone you know who does not know the Lord? Have you thought about sharing your faith with them, but then backed away because you felt you did not have the answers?

Telling people about their need to acknowledge Jesus Christ as their personal Lord and Savior is no easy matter. Nearly everyone who has attempted to witness for Jesus Christ has met opposition of one kind or another.

Some people will respond by saying that Christianity is a faith for weak-minded individuals. Others proclaim that the road that Jesus instructed us to walk is too narrow. Some even suggest that people who literally follow the words of Jesus are old-fashioned and out-of-step with contemporary society. Doubts, excuses, outright rejection and even hostile opposition may be offered by those who refuse to accept the Gospel.

But such is the nature of the battle. Remember, it is not up to us to make people believe. It is simply our task to sow seeds of truth. The harvest is God's responsibility.

THE "HOW TO" FORMULA

Most of us like to find quick and easy solutions for our problems. Books and seminars offering instant success for almost any need are plentiful. You may find some "how to" suggestions for Christian witnessing as you read this book; however, there are no guarantees. Witnessing is a process that involves people in partnership with God. The Bible itself gives us valuable principles and guidelines, but the keys to successful evangelism are not held in our human hands.

There are two major factors to consider when it comes to evangelism: one involves human effort in presenting God's Word, and the other depends on the Holy Spirit. As Jesus said, "No man can come to me, except the Father which hath sent me draw him: and I will raise him up at the last day" (John 6:44). This drawing that the Father does is the work of the Holy Spirit and is paramount, as human effort alone will not bring one to Christ. The "how to" aspect of witnessing found in the following pages refers only to the human factor in Christian witnessing. The rest is up to Him.

MOTIVATION FOR ACTION

The Bible teaches there are two categories of people: those who are perishing and those who are not. The apostle Paul, when writing to the people of Corinth, could not have made it clearer: "For the preaching of the cross is to them that perish foolishness; but unto us which are saved it is the power of God" (1 Corinthians 1:18).

It is not a pleasant thought to think about friends, relatives, and loved ones who belong to the category of the "perishing." The decision they make about the Cross will determine where they spend eternity.

When writing to the believers in Thessalonica, Paul created a vivid description of what happens to those who willingly reject God's plan of salvation for man. He stated:

> And to you who are troubled rest with us, when the Lord Jesus shall be revealed from heaven with his mighty angels, In flaming fire taking vengeance on them that know not God, and that obey not the gospel of our Lord Jesus Christ: Who shall be punished with everlasting destruction from the presence of the Lord, and from the glory of his power. (2 Thessalonians 1:7-9)

Do you know someone who is perishing? Have you taken the time to consider the consequences they will eventually and inevitably face? Take a moment right now and ask God what you can do to share the Good News of our Lord Jesus with them or with others like them. How wonderful it is to be a person God can use as a vehicle to share the message of salvation that will guide a lost soul into eternal life! The way of salvation is the most loving gift anyone can offer.

—3—

GOOD NEWS, BAD NEWS

Approximately two thousand years ago, an angel of the Lord appeared to some frightened shepherds while they were watching their flocks at night. The angel proclaimed:

> Fear not: for, behold, I bring you good tidings of great joy, which shall be to all people. For unto you is born this day in the city of David a Saviour, which is Christ the Lord. (Luke 2:10-11)

This is not just the text from a Christmas card. The message the angel proclaimed to the shepherds watching their flocks near Bethlehem some two thousand years ago, is the very same one that you and I should be proclaiming today.

WHERE IT ALL BEGAN

The relationship between God and mankind began when all things were created, as recorded in the book of Genesis. The Bible states:

> And God said, Let us make man in our image, after our likeness: and let them have dominion over the fish of the sea, and over the fowl of the air, and over the cattle, and over all the earth, and over every creeping thing that creepeth upon the earth. So God created man in his own image, in the image of God created he him; male and female created he them. (Genesis 1:26-27)

The second chapter of Genesis provides additional information in relation to the creation process that God used. Moses, the author of Genesis, continues:

> And the Lord God formed man of the dust of the ground, and breathed into his nostrils the breath of life; and man became a living soul. (Genesis 2:7)

So God created man with a physical body, but man also has a soul and an eternal spirit. The body is the physical frame (the tent or home) that contains the remaining parts of the human, the soul and the spirit.

Although the body is materialistic and can be observed by our senses, the soul is not a physical entity that we can see. The soul encompasses a person's innermost thoughts and feelings. The human soul consists of the mind, the will, and the emotions. But the spirit is the most vital component of the human being where the God of the universe imparted a likeness of Himself into man allowing God and man to share in a relationship together having the qualities of love, devotion, and caring for each other. So man was able to commune with God in a beautiful, harmonious relationship.

However, the prospect of remaining in this beautiful relationship with God was dependent on man's trust and obedience to Him. God created Adam and Eve with a free will because otherwise they would be little more than puppets doing things by compulsion and not be choice. For there to be a love relationship shared, the participants must have the freedom to give and respond to each other by choice. Love cannot be forced or manipulated, so God gave Adam and Eve the ability to respond to His love for them according to their own free will.

Adam and Eve chose not to trust and obey God, and as a result, their choice to be disobedient was a choice that affected not only their own lives but also the lives of every human being born thereafter.

THE FALL OF MAN

The choice to reject God's plan for man was not just a human decision. Adam and Eve were encouraged by the devil himself. The Bible reveals that Satan's rebellion against God took place prior to the fall of man when, as the angel Lucifer, he first had the idea to overthrow God's authority. And in his rebellion, a third of the angels fell with him.

Later as Satan, he fully understood the consequences of his rebellion and put his plan into action. He appeared to Eve in the Garden of Eden in the embodiment of a serpent and promised Eve personal godhood if she willfully disobeyed God (Genesis 3:1-6). Satan's master plan was to thwart God by taking mankind with him to an eternity in Hell (Matthew 25:41).

Through Adam and Eve's disobedience, sin was introduced into the human race. Sin, defined as rebellion against God, brought about the fall and the curse upon humanity. As Paul wrote in the book of Romans:

> Wherefore, as by one man sin entered into the world, and death by sin; and so death passed upon all men, for that all have sinned. (Romans 5:12)

As well, man became spiritually dead. As Paul stated in 1 Corinthians 2:14:

> But the natural man receiveth not the things of the Spirit of God: for they are foolishness unto him: neither can he know them, because they are spiritually discerned.

GOD'S ALTERNATIVE PLAN

Even though God gave free will to man and man fell, God's sovereignty is not affected by the weaknesses of men, nor is it threatened by the clever schemes of the devil. Although Satan, our adversary, is "a roaring lion, [who] walketh about, seeking whom he may devour" (1 Peter 5:8), God is still on the throne. In spite of Satan's devious plan, the Creator of the universe had already established an alternative.

Once again, the words of the apostle Paul provide the best explanation:

> Therefore as by the offence of one judgment came upon all men to condemnation; even so by the righteousness of one the free gift came upon all men unto justification of life. For as by one man's [Adam's] disobedience many were made sinners, so by the obedience of one [Jesus] shall many be made righteous. (Romans 5:18-19)

Then, in one short verse, Paul summarizes the Good News eloquently:

> For the wages of sin is death; but the gift of God is eternal life through Jesus Christ our Lord. (Romans 6:23)

Is there any way to misunderstand God's alternative plan for mankind? The Creator Himself came to this earth and lived a life as a man. And throughout His life here on earth, He never sinned. We as humans could not live perfectly, but He did. Then, fulfilling the prophecy of Isaiah 53:1-12, His life was sacrificed on the Cross. He died as a sacrifice for all our sins.

Whoever believes that Jesus is God, that He died for our sins, and was resurrected to life by the power of His Father, receives a restored, loving, harmonious relationship with the Creator—a relationship that will last forever.

THE GOSPEL IN A SINGLE VERSE

The Old Testament is filled with promises about the coming of the Messiah. It states again and again that He will bridge the gap between God and man. The prophets were not only called by God as watchmen to warn of impending doom, but they were also messengers of hope, proclaiming to the people that God would eventually provide a way out.

Even before God had physically sent His Son Jesus to be the ultimate sacrifice for the sins of man, Isaiah foresaw Him:

> Surely he hath borne our griefs, and carried our sorrows: yet we did esteem him stricken, smitten of God, and afflicted. But he was wounded for our transgressions, he was bruised for our iniquities: the chastisement of our peace was upon him; and with his stripes we are healed. All we like sheep have gone astray; we have turned every one to his own way; and the Lord hath laid on him the iniquity of us all. (Isaiah 53:4-6)

Reflecting the miraculous fulfillment of Isaiah's prophecy, we find another Scripture in the New Testament that triumphantly announces the results of Christ's sacrificial death:

> For God so loved the world, that he gave his only begotten Son, that whosoever believeth in him should not perish, but have everlasting life. (John 3:16)

Recalling my own childhood days, I can remember exactly when this verse became part of my vocabulary. At the time, my motive for memorizing Bible verses was nothing more than to receive a prize from a Sunday School teacher. Consequently, the real meaning of this verse escaped my notice. It was some twenty years later that the impact of the words jolted me into reality. Through this single Scripture, the God of the Bible revealed Himself to me, and I was introduced to His Son, Jesus Christ. From that time forward, my life has never been the same.

What is there about this single verse that has changed so many lives? Anyone who has experienced a life-changing experience with God will answer emphatically: "It's not the verse itself that transforms lives; it is the Author of the verse, the One who

WHOEVER BELIEVES THAT JESUS IS GOD, THAT HE DIED FOR OUR SINS, AND WAS RESURRECTED TO LIFE BY THE POWER OF HIS FATHER, RECEIVES A RESTORED, LOVING, HARMONIOUS RELATIONSHIP WITH THE CREATOR—A RELATIONSHIP THAT WILL LAST FOREVER.

composed it, Jesus Christ." Those who trust and believe in Him are suddenly brought into the kingdom of light, establishing a relationship with God that will last forever and ever. The Gospel, as recorded in John 3:16, describes the greatest love story in the history of our planet.

A HIGH PRIORITY

Jesus placed a high priority on sharing the "Good News." In fact, the topic of witnessing was the central theme of the farewell speech He delivered before He ascended into Heaven. Just before He departed, Jesus was asked if this was the time that the kingdom would be restored to Israel. He stunned those there that day by refusing to answer their question and said:

> It is not for you to know the times or the seasons, which the Father hath put in his own power. (Acts 1:7)

Then focusing their attention on the priority issue for every believer, Jesus stated:

> But ye shall receive power, after that the Holy Ghost is come upon you: and ye shall be witnesses unto me both in Jerusalem, and in all Judæa, and in Samaria, and unto the uttermost part of the earth. (Acts 1:8)

After He had said these things, Jesus was lifted up, as the apostles gathered on the Mount of Olives looked on. Jesus chose the topic of sharing the Gospel with others as the very last thing He proclaimed before physically departing this earth some two thousand years ago. That should be incentive enough for us to be obedient to His words until He returns.

A PATTERN FOR ACTION

Not only did Jesus commission His disciples, but He also gave them a plan of action. His short message about witnessing was centered around the mechanics of how and where witnessing was to proceed.

He said that the first priority was at home, which, for most, was the city of Jerusalem. The next phase of the witnessing process was to proceed to the surrounding area of Judea and Samaria. The final phase was to reach out far beyond these regions "unto the uttermost part of the earth" (Acts 1:8).

The words Jesus proclaimed that day were not just for those present at His ascension. These same words echo down through the many generations of time. The command is for all believers. Even to you and me today.

- Begin by sharing the Good News at home.

- Then take the message to your community.

- Finally, spread the Gospel to the world.

FISHERS OF MEN

While He was still teaching His followers, Jesus made it clear that if they would follow Him, He would give them the necessary guidance they needed to reach the lost.

It is important to realize that although presenting the Good News requires human effort, if the human effort is not inspired by the Holy Spirit and done according to God's will, it may well be done in vain.

The fifth chapter of Luke gives us an interesting scenario which helps demonstrate this principle. As the chapter begins, we are told that many people had gathered around Jesus as He was proclaiming the Word of God. He stood beside a lake where Simon and some others had just finished a fishing expedition that had lasted all night. Their two fishing boats were docked at the edge of the lake, and the men were on the shore washing their nets, preparing them for another day.

In order to distance Himself slightly from the multitudes, Jesus got into one of Simon's fishing boats and asked him to move it out a little way from the shore. From the boat, Jesus began to teach. Then, when He had finished speaking, He said to Simon:

> Launch out into the deep, and let down your nets
> for a draught. (Luke 5:4)

Simon, a professional fisherman, was not especially impressed by what Jesus wanted him to do. He reluctantly said:

> Master, we have toiled all the night, and have taken
> nothing: nevertheless at thy word I will let down
> the net. (Luke 5:5)

Being obedient to what Jesus had instructed brought tremendous results. The Bible states:

And when they had this done, they inclosed a great
multitude of fishes: and their net brake. And they
beckoned unto their partners, which were in the
other ship, that they should come and help them.
And they came, and filled both the ships, so that
they began to sink. (Luke 5:6-7)

Obviously, this illustration relates to fishing for fish, not
for men. However, the significance of this illustration should
be clear. As fishers of men, the important factor is not how
hard we work, or how long we persevere. The issue is how well
we listen. As you are listening, be aware that God may speak
to you in the most unexpected ways.

TWO ROADS TO ETERNITY

It was another one of those unforgettable moments, which
happened while I was attempting to board a downtown
Moscow Metro train during rush hour. As I was getting off the
escalator, trying to make my way towards the boarding area,
several thousand people on both sides of me were pushing and
shoving in opposite directions.

For an instant, I was panic-stricken. Would I be trampled
underfoot? If I stumbled and fell, what would happen to me?
Fear momentarily gripped me. Refusing to give in, I continued
in the direction I was going.

Suddenly, my thoughts were transformed beyond the
present situation. The faces that passed by me on both sides
were blank, without expression. Where were all these people
going? What would they find there when they arrived?

My mind was bombarded with a myriad of thoughts, like countless snowflakes striking a window during a snow storm. Compassion and a sense of urgency flooded my mind as I thought about the millions of people on the wide road headed toward Hell.

Jesus proclaimed there are two widely-contrasting paths leading to the eternal destination of mankind:

> Enter ye in at the strait gate: for wide is the gate, and broad is the way, that leadeth to destruction, and many there be which go in thereat: Because strait is the gate, and narrow is the way, which leadeth unto life, and few there be that find it. (Matthew 7:13-14)

Yes, the road to Hell is a broad path, and countless people are walking on it. How many of us who are on the narrow way leading in the opposite direction have never made an attempt to shout out words of warning?:

Stop!
Turn around!
You're going the wrong way!

—4—

MESSENGERS ON A MISSION

No matter how good our intentions may be, proclaiming our faith in Jesus Christ to others can be an intimidating experience. We find ourselves backing off, saying "I'm not eloquent enough," or "my mind goes blank every time I'm asked a question." Is it necessary to be a pastor or a Bible-college graduate to qualify to be a witness for Jesus Christ? Or can God use people from all walks of life?

Throughout history, God has always used human messengers to communicate His plan of salvation to the lost. One of the things apparent from the Bible is that God chose ordinary people from a wide variety of backgrounds, without any special credentials, to carry His message. Just like us, the people God chose often thought they were incapable of getting the job done.

Take Moses, for example. According to the account in the book of Exodus, the children of Israel had been in bondage as slaves in Egypt for four hundred years. The Pharaoh and the system he represented had held them captive for centuries.

God appeared to Moses through the burning bush in the wilderness, and said:

> Come now therefore, and I will send thee unto Pharaoh, that thou mayest bring forth my people the children of Israel out of Egypt. (Exodus 3:10)

Moses was quite sure that he was unqualified to perform such a major task. He replied:

> Who am I, that I should go unto Pharaoh, and that I should bring forth the children of Israel out of Egypt? (Exodus 3:11)

Moses' reluctant response and his feelings of inadequacy were not enough to convince God that He had chosen the wrong person. Encouraging Moses further, God said, "Certainly I will be with thee" (Exodus 3:12).

Nonetheless, Moses continued to doubt God's ability to choose the right person for the job. In order to express his view more emphatically, Moses said:

> O my Lord, I am not eloquent, neither heretofore, nor since thou hast spoken unto thy servant: but I am slow of speech, and of a slow tongue. (Exodus 4:10)

God made it clear that he had not chosen His reluctant spokesperson because of Moses' natural ability. Any success that Moses had would only be attributed to a supernatural God. Then God said to Moses:

Who hath made man's mouth? or who maketh the
dumb, or deaf, or the seeing, or the blind? have
not I the Lord? Now therefore go, and I will be
with thy mouth, and teach thee what thou shalt
say. (Exodus 4:11-12)

What an encouragement this conversation should be to each
one of us today. When it comes to our being spokespersons for
God, confidence in our own ability is not a required prerequisite. In fact, trusting in our own strength and ability is the very
thing that often hinders us from becoming true servants of God.

NOT A WARM, FUZZY MESSAGE

Of course, there are no guarantees everyone will applaud
when we tell them about their need for Jesus Christ. Proclaiming the "narrow way" as the only route to God has not
always been received as good news. Nor has the message that
eternal life can be obtained always been grasped with great joy
and happiness. Untold numbers of individuals have sacrificed
their lives for the privilege of being messengers of the Gospel.
Yet, throughout the Old Testament, God chose ordinary people
with no extraordinary talents or abilities to communicate His
message, whatever it cost them.

The prophet Jeremiah is another example. His call and
mission came from God, not from man. As the Bible states,
God appointed Jeremiah as His witness before the prophet
was born:

Before I formed thee in the belly I knew thee;
and before thou camest forth out of the womb I

sanctified thee, and I ordained thee a prophet unto
the nations. (Jeremiah 1:5)

Encouraging Jeremiah further, God said:

Say not, I am a child: for thou shalt go to all that
I shall send thee, and whatsoever I command
thee thou shalt speak. Be not afraid of their faces:
for I am with thee to deliver thee, saith the Lord.
(Jeremiah 1:7-8)

When God called the prophets of old, the message they
were given to proclaim did not always make the recipients feel
warm and fuzzy. It was not a message of "I'm O.K. and you're
O.K." It was a message that burned with fire from the very heart
of God and was targeted toward the rebellious men and women.

Just like people in today's world, the people of the past
had drifted far from God. The prophets were appointed to
challenge them. They were not supposed to be concerned
with whether or not they won the "most-popular-person-of-
the-year award." God used Jeremiah to describe the spiritual
condition of His people:

For the house of Israel and the house of Judah have
dealt very treacherously against me, saith the Lord.
They have belied the Lord, and said, It is not he;
neither shall evil come upon us; neither shall we see
sword nor famine: And the prophets shall become
wind, and the word is not in them: thus shall it be
done unto them. (Jeremiah 5:11-13)

Then came the words of warning the prophet was instructed to deliver:

> Wherefore thus saith the Lord God of hosts,
> Because ye speak this word, behold, I will make
> my words in thy mouth fire, and this people wood,
> and it shall devour them. (Jeremiah 5:14)

Who could blame Jeremiah for feeling somewhat insecure even though God had promised to protect him?

Similar messages were declared by all the other Old Testament prophets. Clearly, the call to be a witness was not a glamorous position. Some of the prophets, like Jeremiah, wept and wanted to die.

PAUL'S CALL TO WITNESS

The book of Acts records Paul's recruitment as a witness. On the road to Damascus, Saul of Tarsus, a hostile persecutor of Jesus Christ and His followers, was miraculously, by the hand of God, transformed into Paul, the courageous and committed evangelist and promoter of Jesus Christ.

Jesus called Paul to be a missionary evangelist. As a former zealous persecutor of Christians, from a human standpoint, Paul hardly seemed like a likely candidate to be chosen to evangelize and win souls for Christ. But God, in His mercy and grace, changed a hater of the Gospel to one who came to love it and was willing to die for it. Paul wrote:

> And I thank Christ Jesus our Lord, who hath
> enabled me, for that he counted me faithful,

putting me into the ministry; Who was before
a blasphemer, and a persecutor, and injurious:
but I obtained mercy, because I did it ignorantly
in unbelief. And the grace of our Lord was
exceeding abundant with faith and love which
is in Christ Jesus. This is a faithful saying, and
worthy of all acceptation, that Christ Jesus came
into the world to save sinners; of whom I am
chief. (1 Timothy 1:12-15)

Paul's Damascus Road experience is a wonderful example of how the Lord can take an unworthy individual and
transform him into a believer to fulfill His purposes. As Jesus
stated to Paul:

But rise, and stand upon thy feet: for I have
appeared unto thee for this purpose, to make thee
a minister and a witness both of these things which
thou hast seen, and of those things in the which I
will appear unto thee. (Acts 26:16)

Jesus then declared the purpose of the witnessing mission:

To open their eyes, and to turn them from darkness
to light, and from the power of Satan unto God,
that they may receive forgiveness of sins, and
inheritance among them which are sanctified by
faith that is in me. (Acts 26:18)

GOD'S PLAN FOR EVANGELISM

I t is interesting to notice that when Paul gave his testimony to King Agrippa how closely he kept Jesus' Great Commission instructions for evangelism. Paul stated:

> Whereupon, O king Agrippa, I was not disobedient unto the heavenly vision: But shewed first unto them of Damascus, and at Jerusalem, and throughout all the coasts of Judaea, and then to the Gentiles, that they should repent and turn to God, and do works meet for repentance. (Acts 26:19-20)

Paul's strategy for witnessing was exactly what Jesus had originally intended: first at home, then to the surrounding area, and finally to the uttermost part of the earth.

Witnesses are human messengers who have a mission. Like the apostle Paul, we should be eager to share the Good News with others who have not yet heard it and been given the opportunity to receive Jesus Christ as their Savior. As believers, we should enthusiastically say:

> For I am not ashamed of the gospel of Christ: for it is the power of God unto salvation to every one that believeth. (Romans 1:16)

It is a joyous thing to see how God delivers sinners "from the power of darkness" and brings them "into the kingdom of his dear Son" (Colossians 1:13).

Unfortunately, in today's highly secular world, many voices are critical of the Gospel. We hear and read many words that would seek to make us ashamed of the truth and reluctant or afraid to share it with others.

FORCES OF OPPOSITION

During Jesus' confrontation with Paul on the road to Damascus, He pointed out that the task of witnessing to unbelievers would be with opposition. Nevertheless, He promised to deliver Paul from those who would be the source of the opposition (Acts 26:17). Of course, we encounter the same kind of opposition even though 2,000 years have passed.

One of the most outspoken and hostile individuals I have ever encountered crossed my path the very first time I spoke publicly in defense of the biblical creation view. The meeting was held in a very small church in a Saskatchewan farming community. At the end of the meeting, the local biology teacher (who had been invited by a student) attacked what I had said and defended her evolutionary view with great zeal. Her comments were so rude and insulting, for several days thereafter, I questioned whether I should continue in ministry.

Of course, there have been many other encounters since but none as devastating as that first experience. Today, as I look back over the many years I have been in ministry, I can see how Satan was attempting to discourage me from continuing my work in obedience to God. In actual fact, every attack simply confirms the scriptural principle that "we wrestle not against flesh and blood." I have learned that men and women who oppose the Gospel with the greatest hostility are usually under conviction from the Holy Spirit.

What a comfort that Jesus' promise to Paul is valid and true for all His followers today: He will be at our side.

CHRISTIANITY UNDER FIRE

Christianity has been under attack ever since the formation of the New Testament church. Yet, despite the various attacks that the church of Jesus Christ has faced, *membership* numbers have continued to advance toward the final accounting. Jesus' words have been proven true: "I will build my church; and the gates of hell shall not prevail against it" (Matthew 16:18).

Now, with the 21st century well under way, Satan's agenda to attack the body of Christ is intensifying. His organized efforts to destroy the church and render the followers of Jesus Christ ineffective accelerate day by day. At the same time, we are living in one of the most exciting periods of Christian history ever known. The Gospel is being proclaimed to more people in more places than ever before. How is it possible to reconcile that these two opposing trends are taking place at the same time?

Once, while speaking at a Bible study, I was challenged along these very lines. I had just completed a slide presentation demonstrating how the New Age movement is making an impact around the world and how occultic and Eastern religious ideas have captured the minds of people in many different countries. As I have been accumulating this research for a number of years, I have a lot of material. When audiences see the deluge of activity happening on a global basis, it can be overwhelming. It tends to leave viewers with a feeling of hopelessness.

After the presentation, a middle-aged man stood up and asked me rather sharply, "I wonder if you could set me straight? Last week, we had a speaker who told us that Christianity has never been stronger than it is today. This man told us that many great and wonderful things are happening in the name of Christ all over the world." Taking a deep breath, he continued, "Now here you are, telling us that the whole world is on the way to Hell. Who is telling us the truth? You, or the speaker we had last week?"

The man had a legitimate question. Is the world "going to Hell in the proverbial hand basket?" Or is God's Holy Spirit bringing many people to the Lord? I believe both trends are happening simultaneously. While God is revealing Himself and people are drawn toward Him, Satan is doing everything in his power to deceive others so they will end up in a lost eternity in Hell. Satan has never changed his plan. He has been doing the very same thing since he introduced himself in the Garden of Eden thousands of years ago.

REASONS NOT TO BELIEVE

As I have already noted, the first woman, Eve, was challenged by Satan's plan. He chose his words with clever manipulation. As Genesis records:

> Now the serpent was more subtil than any beast
> of the field which the Lord God had made. And
> he said unto the woman, Yea, hath God said, Ye
> shall not eat of every tree of the garden? And the
> woman said unto the serpent, We may eat of the
> fruit of the trees of the garden: But of the fruit

of the tree which is in the midst of the garden, God hath said, Ye shall not eat of it, neither shall ye touch it, lest ye die. And the serpent said unto the woman, Ye shall not surely die: For God doth know that in the day ye eat thereof, then your eyes shall be opened, and ye shall be as gods, knowing good and evil. (Genesis 3:1-5)

The central theme of the dialogue between Eve and Satan involved God's Word and Eve's understanding of what God had said. Satan's accusation was extremely deceitful. "God did not *really* say what you thought He said," was Satan's line. That lie brought about the fall of man and the curse upon a perfect creation. That same curse still affects the whole world to this day.

Satan has always counted on human pride as the key to his success in deceiving men and women. This is why so many unbelievers are convinced that the Bible is not God's inspired revelation to man. Instead, they maintain that the Bible, and the words it contains, reflect nothing more than the ideas of mortal men.

However, the apostle Paul stated:

All scripture is given by inspiration of God, and is profitable for doctrine, for reproof, for correction, for instruction in righteousness. (2 Timothy 3:16)

Others who question the literal value of the Bible assert that its words require human interpretation for meaning and understanding. There are a variety of views, these people argue, all within the realm of wide speculation.

Finally, there is a group that mocks and scoffs at the Bible. These individuals consider the Bible to be nothing more than a literary work, having no eternal value. Yet, in spite of this fact, the Bible is still the number-one, best-selling book.

WAS JESUS AN IMPOSTOR?

Even the words of Jesus as recorded in the Bible have come under intense attack in the past several years. According to a group of 200 self-proclaimed "Bible scholars," Jesus Christ did not say eighty percent of what He is quoted as saying in the four gospels of the New Testament. This was the proclamation of "The Jesus Seminar," a conference held in Sonoma, California in March 1992. The group openly claimed their objective was to counteract fundamental Christianity.[1] Seminar participants analyzed the words of Jesus by using a unique voting system. After lengthy discussion periods, the "scholars" were asked to make a decision on the authenticity of Jesus' words by choosing a particular colored bead and dropping it into a ballot box. Red and pink beads were chosen for sayings they determined were possibly authentic; gray and black beads were chosen for sayings they claimed Jesus did not say.

Virtually all of Jesus' words in the Gospel of John received gray and black votes. One of the participants, when interviewed by the *Los Angeles Times*, said that virtually nothing in the Gospel of John goes back to what Jesus actually said.

Another Jesus Seminar participant stated in his interview that the findings of the conference would "feed a hunger which existed in the church."[2] He concluded that "many mainstream Christians can no longer believe the picture of Jesus they got as children."[3]

Curiously, the "hunger" these scholars attempted to feed was prophesied in the pages of the very Bible that they scorned. And since that time, over these past few decades, largely through the emergent church movement, the intensity of the attack against the Bible has quadrupled. In 2 Timothy 4:3-4, the apostle Paul outlines an important sign for the last days:

> For the time will come when they will not endure
> sound doctrine; but after their own lusts shall they
> heap to themselves teachers, having itching ears;
> And they shall turn away their ears from the truth,
> and shall be turned unto fables.

The apostle Peter also has strong words of warning for those who would choose to trust in the foolishness of man's ideas rather than in the wisdom of God's revelation:

> But there were false prophets also among the people,
> even as there shall be false teachers among you,
> who privily shall bring in damnable heresies, even
> denying the Lord that bought them, and bring upon
> themselves swift destruction. (2 Peter 2:1)

Could the words of Paul and Peter be targeted for our generation?

EVERYTHING IS GOD

Besides the continuing assaults on Holy Scripture, another major shift in thinking is taking place. During the 1960s and the 1970s, a popular philosophy stated that "God is dead" and that science and technology would bring utopia to planet Earth. However, now that we have recognized that the by-products of our technology threaten to destroy the earth, there is a completely different popular "wisdom"—the idea that "God is *in* everything" and "everything is God."

According to the *gurus* of this "paradigm shift," there are many ways to God (interspirituality). For the follower of an Eastern religious worldview, everyone has the "potential" to become God. To make the claim that Jesus Christ is "the only way" to God is far too narrow and restricting. What about all the other religions and their genuine efforts to reach God? Shouldn't everyone be open-minded enough to accept them? After all, as participants of this new millennium, are we not all citizens of a global, pluralistic society?

From a Christian perspective, tolerance and human respect for people of other belief systems is one thing, but agreement that everything is God, or that there are various paths to salvation, is quite another. Human effort and good works can do nothing whatsoever to pay the price for Adam's sin. The apostle Paul summarized it well:

> For by grace are ye saved through faith; and that not of yourselves: it is the gift of God: Not of works, lest any man should boast. (Ephesians 2:8-9)

That is why Christianity stands separate from all other world religions. Christianity is a relationship, not a ritual. Christianity recognizes the holiness of God, not the righteousness of man. Christianity is a very narrow way. It is *the* way, not *a* way!

NO CHRISTIANITY WITHOUT CHRIST

There are many attacks upon the faith from outside the church's four walls. But perhaps the greatest threat to Christianity can be found within Christianity itself, a form of Christianity that exists without Christ. Over the past several decades, there has been a strong inclination within certain churches to dilute the message of salvation which Jesus so clearly proclaimed.

Nearly two thousand years ago, the term Christian was coined to describe those committed to following Jesus Christ. Christians acknowledged that Jesus had died for the sins of mankind. They believed He was God, incarnate as a man. They believed that if they repented from their sins and acknowledged His death on the Cross and His victorious resurrection, they could be reconciled to God.

Today, the word *Christian* has a far less specific meaning. It can describe all sorts of behaviors, factions, and rites. The name Christianity has taken on many variations. It is used to identify every imaginable sort of religious individual, even though at the most casual observation, these "Christians" are revealed to be nothing more than charlatans and frauds.

The Bible predicts that this will be a common scenario in the "last days." Regarding apostasy in the church, Paul wrote:

> Now the Spirit speaketh expressly, that in the latter
> times some shall depart from the faith, giving
> heed to seducing spirits, and doctrines of devils.
> (1 Timothy 4:1)

Indeed, Christianity, as Paul predicted, has been afflicted by "doctrines of devils." For example, a major sector of Christianity has rejected outright the overwhelming evidence that confirms God's creation. Instead, it has accepted humanistic, atheistic reasonings and philosophies of man.

To make matters worse, many who proclaim themselves to be Christian are much more zealous about worshipping the creation than the Creator. They endorse the religious practices of pagans rather than proclaim the Good News that Jesus Christ died to save us from our sins and give us the hope of eternal life.

To truly understand what it means to be a Christian, the foundational doctrine of the Gospel cannot be compromised or watered down; our salvation depends totally upon placing our faith and trust in the finished work of the Cross. There is no other way to inherit eternal life.

Our first responsibility is to firmly grasp and believe this Good News for ourselves, settling it forever in our hearts.

Our next responsibility is to share it with others, sowing the good seeds of the Gospel and praying that God will grant fertile soil, germinate the seed of the Word, and bring forth eternal life.

—5—

CREATION EVANGELISM

Seminars and conferences are held all over the world, attempting to come up with the ultimate strategic plan for evangelism. Church boards, Bible schools, and seminaries discuss the matter in meetings that go on for days. Books on evangelism are written, tapes are distributed, brochures are printed. Does anyone have the answer to increase the growth of the Christian church?

The answer to this problem is that there are no human answers. There are no rules or formulas. Only God has the answer and the solution. No matter how many preachers, teachers, or seminary professors attempt to come up with plans and schemes to proclaim the message of eternal hope, the Bible always brings us back to the real issue.

A word of warning from the Scriptures is in order for all who seek a plan for evangelism devised merely upon human understanding. Simply stated, "If God isn't in it, it won't work." But such a statement should not discourage us from looking at God's Word for insight and understanding when it comes to the subject of witnessing. It reveals some valuable precedents.

BEGIN WHERE THE BIBLE BEGINS

The Bible begins with the words, "In the beginning God . . ." (Genesis 1:1). Without God, there is no beginning. When sharing the Gospel and witnessing to our generation, it is often imperative that we present the Gospel by starting where the Bible begins . . . "In the beginning, God." It is easy to assume that unbelievers already have an understanding and belief in the God of the Bible. However, in today's world, where millions of people are following either paganism's well-beaten path to Hell or intellectualism's arrogant dismissal of anything spiritual, such an assumption may be misguided.

To clearly and intelligently present the fact that we need to be saved from our sins, it is usually a good idea to explain to the unbeliever how humankind managed to get into such a deplorable situation in the first place. Without presenting the biblical account that man was created in a perfect, sinless condition, the fall of man and the subsequent sentence of death cannot be understood. However, when the holiness of our eternal Creator God is recognized in contrast with the unholiness of mortal sinful men and women, His gracious and redemptive power becomes a welcome alternative.

MARS HILL WITNESSING

History, archaeology, and the Bible reveal that the people of Athens were very religious. Their lives were consumed with worshipping someone or something. The Areopagus, located on Mars Hill in the ancient city of Athens, was one of the favorite locations where the intellects of the day gathered to discuss their objects of worship. It is interesting to note that the roots of the Greek word *Areopagus* precisely describe the kind of worship happening in this location. *Aareos* means sensual pleasure and *pagus* relates to sorcery and witchcraft.

One day, Paul went to the Aeropagus to witness to the people assembled there. The idol-gods worshipped by the Athenians were everywhere. The Athenians were obsessed with worshipping the right god for the right purpose and were fearful they might inadvertently forget one. With this in mind, they had erected an additional idol which they dubbed "The Unknown God."

The Bible reflects Paul's wisdom as he commented on the Athenians' spiritual-mindedness:

> Ye men of Athens, I perceive that in all things ye are too superstitious. For as I passed by, and beheld your devotions, I found an altar with this inscription, TO THE UNKNOWN GOD. Whom therefore ye ignorantly worship, him declare I unto you. God that made the world and all things therein, seeing that he is Lord of heaven and earth, dwelleth not in temples made with hands. (Acts 17:22-24)

It is interesting to observe how Paul presented the Gospel in this situation. Continuing his Mars Hill crusade, he proceeded to point the Athenians toward the Creator:

> Neither is [God]worshipped with men's hands, as though he needed any thing, seeing he giveth to all life, and breath, and all things; And hath made of one blood all nations of men for to dwell on all the face of the earth, and hath determined the times before appointed, and the bounds of their habitation. (Acts 17:25-26)

Emphasizing the reality of the Creator, Paul went on to say:

> For in him we live, and move, and have our being; as certain also of your own poets have said, For we are also his offspring. (Acts 17:28)

After appealing to their understanding of the existence of the Creator, Paul then dropped a word of warning and a challenge for them to get right with God:

> And the times of this ignorance God winked at; but now commandeth all men every where to repent: Because he hath appointed a day, in the which he will judge the world . . . (Acts 17:30-31)

Paul's message to repent or face God's judgment was then balanced with a beautiful message of hope. He went on to tell the Athenians about God's merciful plan of salvation and that it had been accomplished through the death and the resurrection of Jesus Christ (Acts 17:31-32).

The Bible indicates that Paul's message was received in three different ways. Some began to sneer scornfully, resisting the message completely. Others said, "We will hear thee again of this matter." They wanted more time to consider what had been said. Thirdly, the Bible states that "certain men clave unto him, and believed" (Acts 17:32-34).

TRIBULATION WITNESSING

The Mars Hill crusade was centered around a form of "creation evangelism," a Gospel message that begins with God as the Creator of the world. And this is not the only example in the Bible of how the Good News can be presented effectively by pointing people toward the reality of a Creator. The book of Revelation describes a similar presentation of the Gospel which takes place in the future during the Great Tribulation. In this case, rather than a man speaking to people in a particular city, an angel communicates the truth supernaturally to the whole world.

John described his vision of the angel preaching the eternal Gospel:

> And I saw another angel fly in the midst of heaven, having the everlasting gospel to preach unto them that dwell on the earth, and to every nation, and kindred, and tongue, and people, Saying with a loud voice, Fear God, and give glory to him; for the hour of his judgment is come: and worship him

that made heaven, and earth, and the sea, and the
fountains of waters.(Revelation 14:6-7)

If God used "creation evangelism" in the past, and if
He plans to use it in the future, then surely it should be an
effective means of communicating the Gospel to our own
generation.

THE GREAT CREATION COVER-UP

Christianity and a belief in creation go hand-in-hand. To
say that God used evolution as a method of creating is
very confusing and biblically inaccurate. Unfortunately, many
well-meaning people have been confused by this idea which
is called *theistic-evolution*. It is a way to give credit and honor
to evolutionary humanistic reasoning, while at the same time
expressing a token belief in God.

Despite what we have been told, the founding fathers of
the evolution idea were not overwhelmed by evidence that
caused them to reject the creation view. They had far less
respectable motives. They were looking for a way to explain
away the existence of God, and evolution was an idea that
served their agenda. A brief overview of the foundational
principles of evolution will show there is nothing scientific to
substantiate the idea. In essence, it is a theory without sub-
stance, and it should be declared bankrupt by all those who
know there is a God.[1]

Besides the lack of physical evidence to support
evolution, the concept is absolutely opposed to the very
character of God. According to the Bible, God originally

made all things perfect. Contrary to that, evolution claims that complexity arises out of disorder without any plan or design. Also, the theory of evolution contradicts the second law of thermodynamics which has been proven to demonstrate that everything in the physical universe is moving toward a random state—from order to disorder; so why are we clinging to a theory that contradicts the facts? Many other irreconcilable differences exist between evolution and creation. To begin with, evolution states that millions of generations suffered and died as the fit struggled to climb to the top of the pile. The Bible says that all things were created by a plan and for a purpose, then began to degenerate and die because of a curse that resulted from man's sin.

For many years of my life, I was an unbeliever and a staunch evolutionist. One day, by God's grace, I saw the fallacy of evolution and changed my point of view. Several months later, I became a Christian. Now that I am a Christian, I can see no alternative to the biblical view.

Creation claims that the design and complexity of all living things is the handiwork of a Designer, not an accumulation of mistakes over time. Yet, despite the overwhelming evidence that supports the creation view, it is becoming increasingly difficult to answer the critics of creation who are convinced that the God of the Bible is nothing more than legend and myth.

For the past several decades, opposition to a biblical creation view by members of the scientific community has become more outspoken and hostile. A quick survey of several anti-creation books reveals that those who believe in God as the

Creator are categorized as "narrow-minded," "zealous bigots" who are "pseudo-scientific," and "pea-brained."

Today, especially in North America, the agenda to advance the idea of evolution is the number one priority for those who believe in the humanist cause. To be effective witnesses to our generation, it is very important that we are able to confront the fallacy of evolution with some basic undeniable facts about the subject of life's origins.

KEEPING GOD AT A DISTANCE

Trying to point people toward the Creator in a world that has swallowed the dogma of evolution can be an intimidating experience. The subject of origins seems to be a topic that only those with proper training or credentials are capable of discussing. Many people, Christians included, when dealing with the subject of the origin and history of life, have relied upon the speculation of men to supersede the revelation given to us by the God of the Bible.

It is a common myth that scientists are the arbitrators of all truth. Ideally, true science should operate in an environment of open-mindedness and without pre-conceived ideas. Furthermore, for science to work, theories must constantly be re-evaluated. New information that comes to light should always alter old theories.

However, the record shows that the scientific community has not always been as open-minded as it claims to be. When it comes to the well-established *theory* of evolution, few scientists are open-minded at all. For many, evolution has long since passed out of the realm of theory and now is accepted as an established fact. When evidence is presented to the contrary, rather than re-examining the theory, most supporters of evolution simply dismiss the facts as unimportant or say the facts presented are not yet understood in evolutionary terms.

CONFRONTING THE SKEPTICS

First of all, if you are confronted with someone who is skeptical about biblical creation, remember, you do not need a science degree in order to defend your faith in a Creator. All you need is some common sense and logic.

Second, it is important to recognize that most people believe in evolution because they have not carefully considered the facts. They simply believe it because they have been taught that they should believe it. In fact, students of evolution are graded on their science exams on how thoroughly they have believed.

Third, when one presents evidence pointing people toward the Creator, as Paul did on Mars Hill, three responses are possible. Some will sneer and be emotionally hostile. Others may be willing to consider what has been said but not immediately change their view. Some will believe, and their lives will be transformed.

It is imperative to remember as a believer in Christ, the battle you face with those who oppose you is not an intellectual one. Many people have chosen to believe in evolution because they have found it to be a convenient way to distance themselves from God. With this in mind, we should examine some facts that support the creation view.

HOW DID IT ALL BEGIN?

When it comes to discussing the subject of origins, there are basically two views: "In the beginning God" or in the beginning, an explosion took place. According to those who believe in evolution, an intelligent Creator God is not necessary because an explosion adequately explains the origin of all the design and order we observe in the universe.

As we examine some of the contrasting principles between the evolution and the creation views, it is a good idea to review a very significant point. For any model or theory to be credible, it must be backed up and supported by observable evidence. What evidence is there to support the concept of a Creator God? What evidence is there to support the evolutionary claim that an explosion is the creative force behind the origin and development of all things?

Evolution claims that from an original source of matter, everything that exists has had its beginning. It is believed that no designer or intelligence was necessary to bring about the cosmos, the galaxies, our solar system, and all features on the earth, living or non-living.

Evolution theory suggests the universe started out the size of an object no larger than the period at the end of this sentence. From this very minute, very dense piece of matter, everything came into being. If you find this difficult to comprehend, you are not alone. Proponents of evolution suggest that only a few, highly-skilled mathematicians and physicists can understand the complex formulas used to come up with this idea.

Despite the *brilliance* necessary to deduce this amazing theory, few evolutionary theorists have ever asked one very important question. Has anyone ever observed any kind of explosion that has produced any kind of order? Do things proceed in a natural direction from disorder to order? If not, then the foundational principle of evolution is seriously suspect.

Creation claims that an intelligent, eternal being brought all things into existence. The creationist looks at the incredible universe and the design within it and sees the handiwork of God. The creationist believes it takes a great *leap of faith* to reject God as the originator of all things and to adopt an explosion as an alternative.

Of course, the choice to either accept or reject the existence of God is a personal choice that everyone must make. The Bible states:

> O LORD our Lord, how excellent is thy name
> in all the earth! who hast set thy glory above the
> heavens. (Psalm 8:1)

The Psalmist also wrote, "The fool hath said in his heart, There is no God (Psalm 14:1).

Paul's writings state that into every human, an awareness of the existence of God has been encoded (Romans 1:19-20). Reminding people of their choice to accept or reject the evidence that God is the source of all things is a reasonable place to begin when attempting to point people toward the Creator.

THE ORIGIN OF LIFE

A belief in Creation is based on God's revelation to man; evolutionary theory is based on man's speculation which attempts to explain away God. Just as they believe the universe came into existence with a "Big Bang," most evolutionists believe that life emerged from *non-life* hundreds of millions of years ago by a process that cannot be observed today. In general, the "primitive pond" theory suggests that lightning bolts struck a body of water that contained various elements which provided the ingredients for the origin of life. Non-life became life in the prehistoric past, in an unknown place, by a mysterious process not being repeated today. Nevertheless, the certainty with which this happened, it is said, is a fact that cannot be disputed.

There are some serious problems with the idea that life can spontaneously arise from non-life. To begin with, there is no scientific evidence to support the proposition that this can happen. To speculate that life appeared from non-life is one thing. To demonstrate how it happened is quite another. Hundreds of millions of years do not make an impossible idea any more probable.

Most museums, institutes, and universities illustrate the evolution of non-life to life with the use of murals, models, diagrams, and even cartoons. Yet, the fact remains that until a scientific experiment is performed that can show how atoms randomly become complex cells by chance, without any engineered devices designed by intelligent human beings, the whole idea of the origin of life without a Creator is highly questionable.

According to the biblical model of origins, the Creator created life from non-life. It did not happen by chance. Living things came on the scene suddenly. Until the fall of man, all living things were perfect, and there were no flaws. Also, according to the creation model, life was able to reproduce and perpetuate and produce variation according to certain restrictions as determined by the genetic code. The Genesis account states that God said:

> Let the earth bring forth the living creature after
> his kind, cattle, and creeping thing, and beast of
> the earth after his kind. (Genesis 1:24)

Both models—creation and evolution—require a certain amount of faith. The creation model requires less faith. Under no circumstances today does life appear from non-life. Life only comes from pre-existing life. The creation model is credible. It can be supported by observable facts.

THE COMPLEXITY OF LIFE

There is nothing in the universe we have observed that is more complex than life. From the single unit of life called a cell to complex multi-cellular organisms like us, everything we know about life reveals intricate, delicate, masterful design, and planning. It is difficult to understand how anyone could imagine the complexity of life being explained without a Designer. But the fact remains: millions of people worldwide are convinced that a natural process based on randomness has molded and shaped all living things.

Books do not evolve; a book is written by an author. Paintings do not evolve; a painting is painted by an artist. Buildings do not evolve; a building is designed by an architect and constructed by workers. Yet the complexity of life does not require a designer, or so they say! Such a belief requires a great deal of faith.

Think for a moment about the human organs that make up our own bodies. According to evolution, the human eye and the human brain are the product of millions of genetic mistakes that have accumulated over time. Yet no intelligent person would ever suggest that a video camera or a cassette recorder originated and developed without intelligent design.

The perpetuation of life by sexual reproduction is supposed to be the result of billions of slight mistakes in the genetic code that have occurred by chance over millions of years. However, consider the problem associated with this idea. How could complex male and female reproductive systems have originated and developed by chance? The system must be fully developed and functional or reproduction cannot occur.

Until we can illustrate how complex organisms can develop from non-life, then proceed from simple to complex, the whole idea of evolution is nothing more than a fairy tale for adults. While it takes some faith to accept the idea that the complexity of life requires a designer, the evidence is there to support it. It takes blind faith to believe that complex design could happen without a designer when all the evidence makes it impossible, yet millions of people have swallowed it without thinking.

Such was the case in my own life. As a child, I had no reason to question the existence of God. Like most children, I was born a creationist. However, as I studied biology in high school and then in much greater detail later at university, I began to doubt God and then turned to disbelief. I no longer accepted the biblical account of creation as truth. I became an avid supporter of the evolution theory, and in doing so, I distanced myself from God.

It was not until I was thirty years old that my thinking changed. Over a period of several months, I questioned some of the ideas I had just assumed to stubbornly explain away God. Gradually, through a process of facing the facts, which reprogrammed my thinking, I finally rejected evolution and became a creationist, then a biblical creationist. Several months later, I committed my life to Jesus Christ and became a Christian. What happened to me is documented in my biography, *Let There Be Light*, and I have since discovered it happening to thousands of men and women around the world. Many are re-evaluating their former evolutionary ideas and establishing a relationship with their Creator.

THE TIME ELEMENT

It seems extraordinary that an evolutionist who rejects God as Creator has no problem with molecules changing and ultimately developing into human beings. To believe that an explosion + time = life requires faith beyond reason.

Is it logical to say that time is a magical factor? It is easy enough to draw charts depicting fish becoming amphibians, amphibians developing into reptiles, reptiles turning into birds and mammals, and monkeys on their way to becoming men. But, where are the facts to support these ideas?

THE FOSSILS SAY NO

Evolutionists often point to fossils as the proof for the evolution of life. In actual fact, fossils are very supportive of the creation view. There are no fossils that show life in the process of evolving. For example, there are no fish in the process of developing legs, preparing to walk on land. There are no reptiles with their front legs transforming into wings. And, there are no missing links between apes and humans.

In essence, there are no intermediates between species. That is why evolutionists have had to come up with a new mechanism called punctuated equilibrium. This idea suggests that evolution happened very quickly, in rapid bursts. In fact, they say it happened so quickly that no fossils are left behind to show how it happened. But this is really a clever way of dodging the fact that the scientific method is empirical, which means that theories can only be verified by observation or experimentation.

Despite drawings, illustrations, and models, there are no fossils showing how one kind of creature can become another. Furthermore, when we look around the world today at living creatures, nothing verifies the statement that time produces new forms of life. When it comes to demonstrating or documenting the process of evolution, evolutionists must rely upon science fiction, not scientific fact.

GEOLOGY AGREES WITH THE BIBLE

The evolutionary history of life as represented by the geological chart is an idea without evidence. Nowhere on the planet can anyone find the record and sequence of life as described by the geological chart. The only place the chart exists is in a text-book drawing. These drawings have deceived millions of people.

Nor can anyone demonstrate to you how the layers of geological column formed over hundreds of millions of years. The statement that various life forms, represented by the fossils, were gradually buried by some mysterious process that is not happening today, poses yet another problem. When it comes to evolutionary dogma, there are many questions.

The biblical model of the origin and history of life explains why the strata and the fossils formed as they did. The rapid burial of life forms under catastrophic conditions that took place all over the world at a time when the earth was sub-tropical from pole to pole, can easily be understood in light of the Bible's account of the Genesis Flood.

Not only is the biblical creation model credible when it comes to the subject of the origin and history of life; it also answers questions that cannot be explained in another way. When you talk to a skeptic who doubts the Bible's validity regarding the subject of origins, a few simple facts can prove to be valuable information, capable of penetrating his or her armor of disbelief.

THE ORIGIN OF MAN

Everyone has thought about the subject of the origin of man. There are basically two views to explain why we exist. Evolutionists believe our immediate ancestors were brute, ape-like creatures. They say we developed from a lower level of consciousness into the intelligent beings we are to-day. Supposedly our ancestors swung out of trees, lost their tails, and started walking upright on their way to becoming modern man.

Ever since the theory of evolution was popularized by Charles Darwin's *The Origin of Species,* mankind has been obsessed with finding the missing link between ape and man. However, many honest anthropologists will tell you that the missing link between apes and humans is still missing. Although all kinds of ape-human-like creatures have been concocted from the barest of skeletal artifacts, none have stood the test of time. Models, murals, paintings, and text book drawings have been developed from small fragments of skulls, jawbones, knee-joints and even from a single tooth. However, no one has yet uncovered a complete being that remotely proves that our great-great-great-grandparents were monkeys.

Until a complete fossil is found that is part-ape and part-human, scientists committed to Darwin's theory must rely upon inspirational guesswork. As the cover headline of *Discover Magazine*, September 1986, candidly declared:

> We no longer know who gave rise to whom, perhaps not even how, or when, we came into being.

The creationist model proposes that man was made in the image of God, was always superior in intelligence to animals, and that we are not the smartest people who have ever lived. According to the biblical view, original man, despite his fallen nature, could perform and accomplish tremendous things. In Genesis four, we read an account of the many impressive accomplishments from the very dawn of human history. We are told that original man farmed and practiced animal husbandry (Genesis 4:2-3), built cities (4:17), made and played musical instruments (4:21), and even made tools using metallurgical techniques (4:22).

Although original civilizations were destroyed by the worldwide flood, the great civilizations which repopulated the earth, after being scattered from the Tower of Babel (Genesis chapter 11), reveal similar incredible accomplishments. Books on archaeology confirm the Bible's account.

SOWING GOOD SEEDS

There are always two ways to look at the same evidence. In the case of the subject of origins, the two choices are creation or evolution. The question that every open-minded thinker should ask is: which model of origins is the better choice?

When one is witnessing to an evolutionist about the problems that evolution cannot explain, there will be opposition. People who have spent their whole lives in a particular dogma do not easily give up their pride and admit they are wrong. In some cases, the emotional response to a creation perspective is vicious and insulting. It is important to remember that the attacks are not personal. Our battle is "not against flesh and blood" (Ephesians 6:12).

Evolution is a faith just like any other religion. It is faith in man's speculation, and this is the direct result of human rebellion. Some men and women do not want God to be in authority over them, so they simply explain Him away. But all is not lost. Despite human resistance, seeds of truth planted with the direction of God can be fruitful. Only God knows the condition of the soul's "soil." The seeds of truth you sow today, unpromising though they may seem, may be the very seeds of truth that God will choose to germinate tomorrow, bringing forth their fruit in due season.

—6—

EVOLUTION: PHYSICAL OR SPIRITUAL?

The Psalmist wrote, "The secret of the LORD is with them that fear him" (Psalm 25:14), and "The fear of the LORD is the beginning of wisdom" (Psalm 111:10). Truth and wisdom come from God, not from mankind. Trusting in human reason will only lead to false hope and eventual destruction. Rebellion and stubbornness against God will always lead man away from God and ultimately into witchcraft and satanic practices. The prophet Samuel said to King Saul:

> For rebellion is as the sin of witchcraft, and stubbornness is as iniquity and idolatry. Because thou hast rejected the word of the LORD, he hath also rejected thee from being king. (1 Samuel 15:23)

The Bible is full of references and guidelines that vividly warn the reader about the consequences of rejecting the Creator. Paul's letter to the Romans contains such a warning:

> For the wrath of God is revealed from heaven against all ungodliness and unrighteousness of men, who hold the truth in unrighteousness; Because that which may be known of God is manifest in them; for God hath shewed it unto them. For the invisible things of him from the creation of the world are clearly seen, being understood by the things that are made, even his eternal power and Godhead; so that they are without excuse. (Romans 1:18-20)

The evidence for God's existence is unmistakable, and when we willingly reject such overwhelming proof of God's reality, we are without excuse. Professing to be wise, we become fools. Paul's letter to the Romans continues:

> Wherefore God also gave them up to uncleanness through the lusts of their own hearts, to dishonour their own bodies between themselves: Who changed the truth of God into a lie, and worshipped and served the creature more than the Creator, who is blessed for ever. (Romans 1:24-25)

Some of the most difficult confrontations that occur when we are witnessing come from people who once believed in God in early childhood but turned from that faith later in life because of "higher education." I remember one situation that occurred when I was speaking at a meeting held for students and professors at the University of Edmonton, in the province of Alberta.

After I had given a lecture based on the evidence to support creation, I was surrounded by people who had many questions. I could not help but notice one man in his mid-forties. He stood off to the side and waited until the group had dispersed. As he approached me, he was trembling, and when he opened his mouth, he could hardly speak. After stuttering for several moments, he finally got out a few words.

"I've never been more embarrassed in my life," he stammered. "You have completely made a fool of yourself, but worse yet, you have misrepresented Christianity by taking the Bible so literally. In fact, you have insulted my intelligence." His harsh words and his physical appearance were very intimidating.

"What did I say that has made you so angry?" I asked, genuinely puzzled. "I certainly didn't intend to offend anyone, especially someone like yourself who professes to be a Christian. Please explain so I will be able to understand."

The man went on to explain that as a young Christian entering university, he had believed the same kind of "foolishness" that I had taught in my presentation. However, after many years of studying, and three earned PhD degrees, he had discovered that he had been horribly deceived. He had concluded that believing in the Bible was an abomination to his intellect. Now he accepted that science was his authority and was absolutely reliable.

Realizing I was not going to change this man's views, much less convince him that he was wrong, I tried to change the subject. "What church do you attend?" I asked.

"I used to go to a Pentecostal church," he replied, "but now I don't attend any church. I find much more comfort practicing meditation and Yoga. That's where I find real meaning in life." As I shook his hand and left for another appointment, a sorrowful feeling came over me. The man I had been talking with had once worshipped the Creator; now he was deluded into believing a lie. Except for God's grace, I could have been in the very same position, I thought.

When witnessing to people today who have effectively tossed God off the scene, it is helpful to recognize Satan's plan for our generation. Satan, the "god of this world" (2 Corinthians 4:4), has masterminded a plan which he uses to deceive the world. If Satan can entice man to trust in himself rather than being obedient to God, he knows the next step will be the ultimate delusion.

ELIMINATING GOD

Some have said that evolution is nothing more than a good excuse to run away from God. And history confirms that the "religion of evolution" preceded the "theory of evolution" by many centuries. Eastern religions like Buddhism and Hinduism have held to a view that the evolution of consciousness and the development of life from simple forms to complex are the products of time and a mystical guiding force. In fact, this metaphysical concept provided the basis for Darwinian evolution, first published in written form, not by Charles Darwin himself, but by his grandfather, Erasmus Darwin.

During the late 1700s, Erasmus Darwin's contribution to the emerging view of evolution was a two-volume work called *The Zoonomia*. As the leader of a group of humanists, whose goal was to overthrow the widely accepted biblical view, Erasmus Darwin's "Lunar Society" had a primary objective to advance humanism, a religion in which man worships mankind.

By the time Charles Darwin came on the scene, the world was ready for a naturalistic theory to replace the supernatural Creator. The "age of enlightenment" was an era when mankind was ready and willing to throw off the shackles imposed on the human race by man's belief in the Bible and to make the move *onward and upward* toward a human-made Utopia. The only obstacle hindering the "great awakening" was the necessary education of the masses. It did not take long for several volunteers to help disseminate the message.

Karl Marx, given credit as the father of the communist movement, embraced Darwinian evolution with great zeal. Soon, the theory of evolution became a major argument used to advance a view called "scientific atheism." This, in turn, became a compulsory course that shaped the politics and culture of a large part of the planet behind the Iron and Bamboo curtains in the communist world.

Meanwhile, in the western world, evolution was strongly endorsed and advanced by John Dewey, the author of the *Humanist Manifesto*. Once again, the secular educational institutions of a number of nations were sympathetic to the philosophies of men who willingly chose to deny the existence of God.

NOTHING NEW UNDER THE SUN

According to King Solomon, there is nothing new under the sun. History merely repeats itself:

The thing that hath been, it is that which shall be;
and that which is done is that which shall be done:
and there is no new thing under the sun. Is there
any thing whereof it may be said, See, this is new?
it hath been already of old time, which was before
us. There is no remembrance of former things;
neither shall there be any remembrance of things
that are to come with those that shall come after.
(Ecclesiastes 1:9-11)

No words could better describe the history of man. From
the Garden of Eden to the present day, the human race has
insisted upon cooperating with the devil's scheme. Refusing to
place their trust and obedience in God, millions have turned
to the foolishness of men's ideas, then taken the next step and
fallen headlong into Satan's deceptive trap.

THE MORALITY FACTOR

The rejection of God as Creator has an immediate effect on
society. If there is no Almighty Creator, there are no rules,
no morals, and no absolute standards. If man is the highest
product of the evolutionary process, then there is no higher
order than man. If there is no higher order than man, then
man can make his own rules.

But this creates a problem: which man or woman do we
listen to? Which rules are right, and which rules are wrong?
Or, is there such a thing as right, or wrong? Maybe morals
and values are relative, depending on who you are, and where
you live. Humanists' debates go on and on.

In Romans 1, Paul describes just such a conundrum. He wrote:

> And even as they did not like to retain God in their knowledge, God gave them over to a reprobate mind, to do those things which are not convenient; Being filled with all unrighteousness, fornication, wickedness, covetousness, maliciousness; full of envy, murder, debate, deceit, malignity; whisperers, Backbiters, haters of God, despiteful, proud, boasters, inventors of evil things, disobedient to parents, Without understanding, covenantbreakers, without natural affection, implacable, unmerciful: Who knowing the judgment of God, that they which commit such things are worthy of death, not only do the same, but have pleasure in them that do them. (Romans 1:28-32)

Evolution, the most degrading, destructive philosophy in the history of the earth, is a major factor in the self-destruction of humanity.

THE FINAL DELUSION

The Bible teaches that a period of time preceding the second coming of Jesus Christ will be a time of great deception. For the past several centuries, Bible scholars have been searching the Scriptures for tell-tale clues to indicate His imminent return. As we shall soon see, most of them agree that the "signs of the times" reveal that He is coming soon.

One of the well-known prophetic events of the last-days scenario is the appearance of a world leader who will eventually claim to be God. Paul described this individual, commonly known as the "Antichrist," in detail:

> Let no man deceive you by any means: for that day shall not come, except there come a falling away first, and that man of sin be revealed, the son of perdition; Who opposeth and exalteth himself above all that is called God, or that is worshipped; so that he as God sitteth in the temple of God, shewing himself that he is God. (2 Thessalonians 2:3-4)

The power and the deceptive nature of the Antichrist will have a deluding influence of major proportions. Paul further warns:

> Even him [the Antichrist], whose coming is after the working of Satan with all power and signs and lying wonders, And with all deceivableness of unrighteousness in them that perish; Because they received not the love of the truth, that they might be saved. And for this cause God shall send them strong delusion, that they should believe a lie. (2 Thessalonians 2:9-11)

Most Bible-believing Christians agree that at the present time, the world is being conditioned and prepared for the "lie" that Paul warns about. The greatest delusion in the history of mankind is rapidly being spread around the world; the eastern, metaphysical, religious worldview that man can be God is being advanced as the new hope for mankind.

Countless thousands of New Age enthusiasts, gurus, and mystics are proclaiming that mankind is on the verge of a quantum leap of consciousness. According to them, we are on the verge of evolving into gods. One day soon, as Paul forewarned, the Antichrist will make his way upon the scene, bringing this belief to its earth-shattering climax. We are fast approaching the time when history will repeat itself for the last time.

THE LAST NEW AGE

Throughout the world, changes of great magnitude are underway. Some call it another "great awakening." Others have labeled it a "paradigm shift" or a "new millennium" or the dawning of the "age of Aquarius." Whatever the words, they describe a time known as the "New Age," a period of major sociological change that will open the door to the greatest evolutionary "leap of consciousness" the world has ever known. The transition from the physical to the metaphysical, the natural to the supernatural, supposedly promises peace, prosperity, and power.

Many people in the world today are sympathetic to this view. For example, consider the words written by the internationally known psychologist and "human potential" speaker Jean Houston:

> In this time of planetary culture we need the
> full complement of human resources, wherever

they may be found. We need to bring forth and orchestrate all the rhythms of human awakening that have ever been in humanity's search for what it can be.

Whether it be through dancing, drumming, chanting, fasting, or employing the many varieties of psychophysical and psychospiritual exercises, human beings have learned to travel to their edges, there to fall off the known world and bring back news from the unknown. And so we join ancient processes to modern research methods to help elicit various phenomena of consciousness.[1]

How can we explain the profound changes in thinking that have taken place in our global society in such a relatively short period of time? Remember, this is not just the cry of a few crackpots at the fringe of society. These ideas are being presented by mainstream educators and political leaders. A review of a few New Testament Scriptures provides the answer.

For example, Paul told Timothy:

Now the Spirit speaketh expressly, that in the latter times some shall depart from the faith, giving heed to seducing spirits, and doctrines of devils. (1 Timothy 4:1)

Further warning of the seriousness of the situation for followers of Jesus Christ, Paul said:

> Yea, and all that will live godly in Christ Jesus
> shall suffer persecution. But evil men and seducers
> shall wax worse and worse, deceiving, and being
> deceived. (2 Timothy 3:12-13)

The Bible indicates that the return of Jesus Christ will be preceded by a time of great deception. False teachers, false prophets, deceitful spirits, and doctrines of demons will be plentiful. Satan, the "god of this world," has done an effective job of deceiving the masses not only in the past but also right now as we see the revival of occult practices taking place.

A quick review of the Old Testament shows that God does not overlook man's indulgence in satanic witchcraft practices. Specific portions of Scripture reveal the seriousness of God's warnings. For example, when the children of Israel were about to enter the promised land, God made this proclamation:

> When thou art come into the land which the
> LORD thy God giveth thee, thou shalt not learn
> to do after the abominations of those nations.
> There shall not be found among you any one that
> maketh his son or his daughter to pass through
> the fire, or that useth divination, or an observer of
> times, or an enchanter, or a witch. Or a charmer,
> or a consulter with familiar spirits, or a wizard, or
> a necromancer. For all that do these things are an
> abomination unto the LORD: and because of these
> abominations the LORD thy God doth drive them
> out from before thee. (Deuteronomy 18:9-12)

The choice of the word "abomination" that is used three times in this context should make the point clearly. God abhors witchcraft and the various forms of pagan worship it encompasses, whether it took place as an idolatrous ritual in the past, or whether it takes place today in a mindfulness session, a Yoga class, or an energy-healing treatment. Whenever we refuse to listen and obey God's instructions to turn away from such practices, He eventually takes drastic action. Using New Age or spiritual terminology to describe pagan practices does not fool God. He will do what He says He will do. He keeps His Word.

PARADIGM SHIFTS

History reveals that major changes in thought or worldviews occur very slowly. At first, new ideas have little-perceived impact. Then, almost suddenly, old views become obsolete and are replaced by whatever new worldview is being heralded as *the way, the truth, and the life*. In other words, long-held beliefs do not change easily. However, when change does occur, the speed in which it happens is staggering.

For example, one of the most dramatic changes ever to be witnessed in modern times was the incredible collapse of the communist Marxist regime imposed on the former Soviet Union for over seventy years. Throughout those years, belief in God was considered nothing more than a crutch for the weak-minded. God, along with other religious ideas, was forced out of existence and relegated to museums representing the primitive past. Communist leaders proclaimed that modern men and women were now in the position to become masters of the universe. Human effort, brotherhood, and ingenuity would bring forth the Utopia Marx promised.

While humanists were busy marketing the idea that God did not exist and that science and technology were capable of resolving all of our problems, another radical idea was beginning to take root. Around the mid-1960s, missionaries of Eastern religions, better-known as "gurus," were appearing on college and university campuses, making bold new statements. "God is not dead," they said. "God is everything." A number of interested observers, grown weary of materialism's emptiness, were all too willing to listen.

Then came the 1980s and the 1990s. Science and technology had not fulfilled their promises. In fact, the by-products were threatening the very existence of humanity. Humankind's many problems extended beyond the borders of countries, provinces, and states. The list of challenges, called "global crisis situations," had the potential of destroying the human race.

Suddenly, a humanistic plan of salvation for the human race was not as desirable as it had been in the past. Materialistic solutions fell short of the promises given to the previous generation. Assurances of peace, prosperity, and human enlightenment offered by Eastern religions seemed hopeful and worthy of consideration.

MYSTICAL MADNESS

Mysticism for the masses has become a growing trend since the last decade of the twentieth century. The rapid change from physics to metaphysics, has been for the most, an unpredictable phenomenon. But from the Bible's perspective, it should have come as no surprise. The downhill spiral is right on course. Materialism, the product of atheism and humanism, has laid the foundation for the mystical madness that has enchanted our present society.

Curiosity, coupled with the failure of liberal Christianity to satisfy the spiritual needs of our present generation, have been the two greatest factors in our culture's attraction to mysticism. In a world full of cares, frustration, anxiety, and fear, nearly everyone is looking for something that will offer a quick fix, bringing peace, power, and renewed hope.

New thought, new therapies, and new techniques of the New Age claim to provide answers, solutions, or instant remedies for day-to-day troubles. It is sad to say that there is nothing new about any of them. Yet, spiritual enlightenment, a higher dimension of consciousness, physical healing, and relief from anxiety and stress are welcome promises to the spiritually thirsty soul. Self-realization, self-fulfillment, and self-esteem are the building blocks of a modern Tower of Babel, paving the way for a human ascent into godhood. Around the world, countless millions of people are falling into these deceptions.

DOORS TO NIRVANA

The enticing doorways into Satan's realm are many. Yoga and meditation promise to relax the body while, at the same time, link the mind to the universal consciousness. Chanting, breath prayers, centering prayer, contemplative prayer, and deep-breathing exercises are supposed to introduce practitioners to a higher, spiritual plane. Crystals, hallucinogenic drugs, and New Age-type music claim to open the door to a whole new world of understanding. Spirit guides, communicating with the dead, and angelic encounters are said to provide guidance and direction as well as revealing messianic visions of hope for the future.

At first relegated to the "hippie" fringe of society, the New Age movement has now hit the mainstream. Eastern philosophy has infiltrated every aspect of our society. The Hare Krishna promoters of the 1960s came up with a new approach. Rather than shaving their heads, wearing strange clothes, and chanting, they have changed their agenda. Now many have become deans, department heads and professors in major colleges and universities. The former Judeo-Christian worldview and traditional view of God as Creator has been replaced by an Eastern view that teaches that God is everything and that even man can become God.

The quantum leap to higher consciousness is within the grasp of all sincere seekers of the New Age lie. As Satan said to Eve, "ye shall be as gods" (Genesis 3:5).

THE QUANTUM LEAP

Remember, when you talk to a New Ager, the promise of godhood is very appealing to the unbelieving mind. For one thing, there is no understanding of the need to repent from sin. As well, human nature in its fallen condition has always desired to seek fame, fortune, and, of course, power. Even the slightest success in these areas can fuel the fire to attain an elevated human potential.

From an Eastern, metaphysical worldview, the leap to higher consciousness and the self-realization of godhood is a natural step in the progression of life. According to one of the basic beliefs of metaphysics, molecules have become men over millions of years, and evolution has been the guiding force that has paved the way. In essence, evolution is a mystical force that connects everyone and everything.

In the Western world, long-steeped in a tradition of Judeo-Christian theology, evolution has had a much more subtle effect. Evolution, a natural process, is understood as the "scientific" reason we are here. It has, for all practical purposes, removed the need for God as the Creator.

Inevitably, an Eastern and a Western worldview have joined forces, so that the phrase "never the twain shall meet" is no longer true. Spiritual gurus from the East, and the scientific "free-thinkers" from the West are discussing how their two world views are interrelated. Science and religion have joined hands.

As an example, consider a statement by Dr. Brian O'Leary in his book called *Exploring Inner and Outer Space, A Scientist's Perspective on Personal and Planetary Transformation:*

> In the new physics, mind meets matter, East meets West, yin meets yang, psychology meets physics, and mathematics meets mysticism. We are inevitably pulled toward the middle of the graph where we begin to understand the myths, metaphors, and practices of the mystical traditions of the Far East at the same time that we reach into the laws of matter.[2]

The impact of such an idea on modern society is apparent. Evolution has removed the need for God. Evolution is the galactic force that connects all things together. Evolution provides a way for man to become God. It sets us up for the greatest delusion in the history of our earth, a period described in the Bible as the "last days."

GOD'S PERSPECTIVE

In the book of Exodus, God gave the Ten Commandments through His servant Moses. In the first commandment, we read:

> Thou shalt have no other gods before me. Thou shalt not make unto thee any graven image, or any likeness of any thing that is in heaven above, or that is in the earth beneath, or that is in the water under the earth: Thou shalt not bow down thyself to them, nor serve them: for I the LORD thy God am a jealous God, visiting the iniquity of the fathers upon the children unto the third and fourth generation of them that hate me; And shewing mercy unto thousands of them that love me, and keep my commandments. (Exodus 20:3-6)

Is it not obvious that God wants our individual attention? Any less than wholehearted devotion to Him will not do. No wonder the prophets begged the apostate people of their generation to turn back to God. The prophet Jeremiah pleaded:

A conspiracy is found among the men of Judah, and among the inhabitants of Jerusalem. They are turned back to the iniquities of their forefathers, which refused to hear my words; and they went after other gods to serve them: the house of Israel and the house of Judah have broken my covenant which I made with their fathers. Therefore thus saith the LORD, Behold, I will bring evil upon them, which they shall not be able to escape. (Jeremiah 11:9-11)

As Christian believers, it is our responsibility to tell people about the truth. If we know what God's perspective of the New Age is, should we not be willing to tell others who do not know? The call of Jeremiah to the people of his day should be our call to our generation: Turn your back on the gods of this world! Turn back to the One who created you!

—7—

SIGNS OF THE TIMES

How much do unbelievers know about the prophetic accuracy of the Bible? Not much at all. Yet, one of the unique qualities of Christianity is the claim that Scripture foretells certain things about the future with one-hundred-percent accuracy. For this reason, biblical prophecy can open doors of conversation when you are attempting to present the Gospel.

During Old Testament times, the litmus test for prophetic insight was perfection. Any less than a perfect record for a prophet meant that he was a fraud, and according to the law, he deserved to be stoned to death. (Certainly, such a stiff test would quickly end the careers of some of today's self-proclaimed prophets and prophetesses.)

For that reason, the Bible's prophecies can be trusted. If they have not already been fulfilled, they will be some day. The apostle Peter encouraged believers to investigate what God has foretold:

> We have also a more sure word of prophecy;
> whereunto ye do well that ye take heed, as unto a
> light that shineth in a dark place, until the day dawn,
> and the day star arise in your hearts. (2 Peter 1:19)

COFFEE SHOP EVANGELISM

For years, I have had a daily habit of waking up early in the morning, going to a nearby restaurant for a cup of coffee, and reading the daily newspaper. Keeping up with current events in light of the Bible has always been one of my passions since becoming a Christian.

For a period of several weeks, an unusual number of current events were reported in the *Los Angeles Times* that related to the Bible's "last days" predictions. Each morning, when I saw an article that interested me, I would tear the page out of the paper, take it to my office, and file it there.

After observing what I was doing for several mornings, a waitress expressed her curiosity while she re-filled my coffee cup. "Could you tell me," she politely inquired, "why you come in here every morning and rip up the newspaper?"

Somewhat embarrassed, I told her I was collecting articles on current events for a seminar that I present. She became even more curious. "What kind of a seminar?"

I briefly told her about my ministry called Understand The Times in which I use the Bible as my text, evaluating current trends and also providing insights for the future.

The young lady seemed surprised. "The Bible? You mean the Bible has something to say about what's going on in the world today?" she asked. "I never knew that before!"

Many people do not realize that the Bible is a key to understanding the past, present, and future. Obviously, every detail of every current event is not predicted in Scripture. Nevertheless, God's Word certainly helps us analyze what is happening, why these things are happening, and where we are headed in the future.

My experience and the experience of others has been consistent. When unbelievers find out that the Bible gives insights about today's events and tomorrow's world, they may also be willing to consider what it has to say about spiritual truths. When you witness to people who have not accepted Jesus Christ as their Lord and Savior, showing them biblical insights for contemporary issues can initiate interesting conversations.

PROMISE OF A COMING SAVIOR

Throughout the Old Testament, more than 300 prophecies were given by the prophets predicting that the Messiah, the Savior of the world, would come. Around 2000 years ago, meeting the demands of the Scriptures that prophecy must be one-hundred-percent accurate, Jesus Christ came and fulfilled these prophecies.

Moses declared that the coming Messiah would be from the tribe of Judah (Genesis 49:10).

The prophet Micah foretold that He would be born in the city of Bethlehem (Micah 5:2).

Isaiah stated that He would come from the family line of Jesse, the father of King David (Isaiah 11:1).

Jeremiah predicted the Messiah would come from David, one of Jesse's eight sons (Jeremiah 23:5-6).

Not one of these is a vague or ambiguous prediction. We could also look at some of the accurate statements that King David made about the coming Messiah's death, predictions he made approximately 1000 years before the birth of Jesus. Although crucifixion was unknown as a means of capital punishment at the time, David vividly described the death of Jesus upon the cross. He stated:

> I am poured out like water, and all my bones are out of joint: my heart is like wax; it is melted in the midst of my bowels. My strength is dried up like a potsherd; and my tongue cleaveth to my jaws; and thou hast brought me into the dust of death. (Psalms 22:14-15)

Every one of the 300 Old Testament messianic prophecies has been accurately fulfilled. The Bible said that the Messiah would come, and He came. Why should we suppose that the prophecies regarding His second coming are not also true?

HE'S COMING AGAIN

On one occasion, the Pharisees and Sadducees asked Jesus to show them a sign from Heaven. Jesus answered and said to them:

> When it is evening, ye say, It will be fair weather:
> for the sky is red. And in the morning, It will be
> foul weather to day: for the sky is red and lowring.
> O ye hypocrites, ye can discern the face of the
> sky; but can ye not discern the signs of the times?
> (Matthew 16:2-3)

Whether or not Jesus will return in the future is not a valid question. This question has already been answered clearly in the Scriptures. When He ascended into Heaven, two angels stood by and proclaimed to all those there:

> Ye men of Galilee, why stand ye gazing up into
> heaven? this same Jesus, which is taken up from
> you into heaven, shall so come in like manner as
> ye have seen him go into heaven. (Acts 1:11)

When unbelievers are skeptical of the Bible, words like these do little to convince them that Christ's return is certain. In fact, the apostle Peter pointed out that before the second coming, scoffers will reject the idea that Jesus will ever return. This will be one of the signs that the second coming is near. As Peter forewarned:

> Knowing this first, that there shall come in the last
> days scoffers, walking after their own lusts, And
> saying, Where is the promise of his coming? for since
> the fathers fell asleep, all things continue as they were
> from the beginning of the creation. (2 Peter 3:3-4)

There are many scoffers in the world today. There is also an abundance of false prophets and false teachers who claim they have a "hot line" with God and know the exact day and hour that Jesus will return. To this particular "last days" phenomenon, Jesus said:

> But of that day and hour knoweth no man, no, not the angels of heaven, but my Father only. (Matthew 24:36)

Jesus did say, however, that we can know the season of His second coming. In order to emphasize the importance of being ready for His return, Jesus gave the following parable:

> Now learn a parable of the fig tree; When his branch is yet tender, and putteth forth leaves, ye know that summer is nigh: So likewise ye, when ye shall see all these things, know that it is near, even at the doors. (Matthew 24:32-33)

Have you noticed? The signs of the times do indicate that Jesus is right at the door! Of course, we need to be cautious and pray for godly wisdom to keep us from becoming so focused on seeing prophecy fulfilled and the Lord's return that we neglect to do the work He has commissioned us to do. But a scriptural understanding of end-times signs can help stir our enthusiasm and can be a very useful way to share our faith in Jesus Christ with skeptical unbelievers.

SIGNS OF THE TIMES

One day, as Jesus was on the Mount of Olives, the disciples came to Him and privately asked Him this question:

> Tell us, when shall these things be? and what shall be the sign of thy coming, and of the end of the world? (Matthew 24:3)

In response, Jesus mentioned several events that will herald His return. He spoke of false teachers and false christs who will come in His name and have the power to deceive many (Matthew 24:5, 23-24). Jesus mentioned there will be wars and rumors of wars, and that nations will rise up against other nations (Matthew 24:6-7). He said famines and earthquakes will be common (Matthew 24:7). He said to expect lawlessness and cruelty of people against others (Matthew 24:12). He said another indicator of His imminent return is that the Gospel will be proclaimed to all nations as a witness, and then the end will come (Matthew 24:14).

LAST DAYS WITNESSING

A number of years ago, I spoke at a conference in St. Petersburg, Russia. During this time, God gave me a wonderful opportunity to see first-hand how biblical insights for contemporary issues can have an impact on reaching lost souls.

Svetlana was a middle-aged lady who oversaw the lecture theater where I was speaking. She had been sitting in on our Bible study lectures every day as an observer. Early in the week when the lectures began, judging by her expression and body language, she seemed somewhat skeptical and disinterested. However, as the week of presentations proceeded, her attitude started to mellow.

On the last day of the study, I was making a slide presentation illustrating why I believed we could be living in a period which the Bible calls the last days. Using Scriptures and current events, I presented the biblical view that the return of Jesus Christ could be close at hand. The people in attendance were intensely interested in the topic.

During the concluding prayer, I felt a slight tap on my shoulder. Looking to my left, I saw one of the Russian translators leaning towards me. He whispered, "There's a lady who has walked up from the back of the room who wants to ask the Lord to come into her life." I looked up and saw Svetlana standing to my left with tears in her eyes. What a joyous time we experienced as she prayed aloud before the entire group.

MORE SIGNS

Not only did Jesus Himself indicate that His second coming will be preceded by a number of prophesied events. Others did as well. Old Testament prophets told of signs that will identify the last days. New Testament writers also forewarned of events that will precede the second coming of Jesus Christ.

Among the most common themes of the "last days" scenario is the appearance of a one-world governing system, global economy, and a one-world religion, all under the leadership of a man—the Antichrist—who claims his divinity. Properly documenting these themes from the Bible is beyond the scope of this particular book, and other books have already been written which present this subject with supporting Scriptures.

Over the past several years, the number of events that line up with the political and religious system of the Antichrist have become very obvious and cannot be denied. But not only do the events line up politically, economically, and religiously, many other events going on today are also right on target morally and socially. The whole world is under siege. In the words of Jesus:

> And as it was in the days of Noe, so shall it be also in the days of the Son of man. They did eat, they drank, they married wives, they were given in marriage, until the day that Noe entered into the ark, and the flood came, and destroyed them all. Likewise also as it was in the days of Lot; they did eat, they drank, they bought, they sold, they planted, they builded; But the same day that Lot went out of Sodom it rained fire and brimstone from heaven, and destroyed them all. Even thus shall it be in the day when the Son of man is revealed. (Luke 17:26-30)

What was it like in the days of Noah and the days of Lot? Immorality, sexual perversion, wickedness, and violence, which are so prevalent in *our* world were rampant in those days as well. The similarities are shocking and clearly indicate we are living in the very environment Jesus predicted will exist before His return. There is no question about the events that are coming. The question is, are we prepared for them? Have we done all that we can do to prepare others?

ALERTING THE LOST

There is urgency in the air. Unbelievers are destined for Hell, and they may get there much sooner than we care to think. Have we made every effort to warn them about their destiny? It is vital that we consider our most important calling as Christians. Remember the words of Jesus, "ye shall be witnesses" (Acts 1:8). The responsibility we have is indisputable, and the time left for witnessing is running out.

It is helpful to use a metaphor to depict the urgency of alerting the lost to the coming judgment of God. We are like a person who sees a house on fire and knows that people are asleep inside. Only a very callous, unconcerned person could walk away and not do everything possible to warn the inhabitants of the impending doom.

Warning people about their need for eternal salvation is much more urgent. Perhaps your own mother or father, son or daughter, relative or friend is hopelessly lost on the pathway that leads toward eternal separation from God. The flames of a burning house are insignificant in comparison with the punishment in Hell for those who reject God's gift of salvation.

Now is the time. Today is the day we can pursue witnessing to those who come into our lives. We should prepare ourselves as best we can to reach all those we can, effectively as we can, while we can. Then we must remember again that once we have faithfully sown the seeds, the rest is up to God.

> So then neither is he that planteth any thing, neither he that watereth; but God that giveth the increase. (1 Corinthians 3:7)

—8—

GIVING A REASON

When you are making an effort to reach out to the unsaved, you will want to be alert to the kinds of challenges you may encounter. There are several common questions, comments, or responses that nearly every outspoken Christian has faced at one time or another. After all, unbelievers must justify their position if they are going to continue to be comfortable in their unbelief. Every skeptic has a defense mechanism or two that he or she constantly uses as a shield against Christianity. Peter wrote:

> But sanctify the Lord God in your hearts: and be ready always to give an answer to every man that asketh you a reason of the hope that is in you with meekness and fear: Having a good conscience; that, whereas they speak evil of you, as of evildoers, they may be ashamed that falsely accuse your good conversation in Christ. (1 Peter 3:15-16)

There is a tendency for us to defend the truth with passion and vengeance. When someone challenges our faith and comes up with arguments that are sarcastic or overtly hostile, we might be tempted to react with knee-jerk retaliation. Sometimes our tone of voice is damaging or insulting. Peter cautions us to present our beliefs in a manner that represents Christ and His character.

With Peter's concerns in mind, I thought it might be helpful to share with you some answers to ten commonly debated issues or arguments against Christianity. I suspect you will hear every one of these arguments more than once when you attempt to witness to our generation.

ARGUMENT NUMBER ONE: CREATION IS A MYTH

To certain individuals, a belief in the God of the Bible as the Creator is ludicrous. Some people claim that only a "nitwit" or a "moron" could set aside all the facts that support the evolutionary view and accept creationism. These people believe that evolution has gone well beyond the parameters of a theory and is now an undisputed fact.

Many Christians, although creationists by belief in their thinking, feel ill-equipped to handle even the slightest attack from an evolutionary opponent. The fear of being intimidated by an expert who claims there is a massive accumulation of information strongly favoring evolution can be a very real barrier. It can keep us from opening our mouths in defense of our Creator.

As we have already seen, the foundational principles of evolution are based far more on *faith* than are the basic principles of creation. Even a limited understanding of facts and some common sense and logic can cause the most stubborn evolutionist to stop and think.

A number of years ago, I was challenged about my creationist beliefs by a lawyer friend. Bill and I had been working together on a project for several years. Although we had spent days and weeks together, I had never felt it appropriate to talk to him about my creation views. Finally, one day the topic surfaced, and I stated my case.

Shocked and somewhat taken aback, my friend blurted out, "I find it hard to believe you are a creationist." Shaking his head, he continued, "I don't know another person who has a university education who claims to believe in creation. You must be kidding me."

Bill was serious about what he had to say. He was convinced that his colleagues and friends with university degrees believed in evolution because they had carefully examined all the evidence and that the evidence proved creation to be a myth. As we sat down at a restaurant table, a simple idea suddenly flashed through my mind. I took my coffee mug, set it in the middle of the table and asked Bill to consider the statement I was about to make. "Let's suppose," I said, "that the cup between us is sitting here because it is the product of millions of years of random chance events. What would you think of my conclusion?"

"I'd say you were absolutely crazy," Bill quickly replied.

"All right," I immediately responded, "look up from the cup about eighteen inches and stare me directly in the face while I ask you another question. Do you think I am sitting here because I am the product of millions and millions of years of random mistakes that accumulated by an evolutionary process?"

For a moment there was silence. I did not need to say another word. The seeds of truth planted that day will always be in my friend's mind.

Over the years, people have written and told me some incredible stories. Often, a particular slide I showed in a presentation or a stated fact they had never before considered got them thinking. Suddenly, their whole evolutionary worldview was shaken. They had to reconsider their position.

While lecturing to a group of intellectuals in Russia, a gentleman approached me. He handed me his business card which indicated he was the head of a department of science at a university. He told me that in his lifetime he had written seven books that had the word "evolution" in the title. With excitement and great enthusiasm, he said, "Tonight, in sixty minutes, I have had questions answered that I was never able to answer before. My whole worldview has been totally shattered." Truly, God's Word and His Truth are sharper than any two-edged sword.

ARGUMENT NUMBER TWO: WORSHIP MOTHER NATURE, NOT FATHER GOD

In December, 1991, I spoke to the Institute for Science and Atheism at the National Academy of Sciences in Moscow, Russia. The meeting was attended by about forty Russian scientists and philosophers who claimed they were devout atheists. In other words, they said they did not believe in the reality of the biblical Creator God.

I had been asked to speak on the subject of evolution as the basis of New Age philosophy. To my surprise, in the question and answer period that followed the lecture, it became apparent that some individuals felt very defensive about my negative statements regarding Eastern mysticism. In fact, it was obvious that this group did not represent an atheistic view at all. They were pantheistic in their beliefs. Some of them suggested that Eastern religious techniques like Yoga and meditation would be a great benefit to their society in the future.

The chairman of the meeting was the most outspoken of all. As he made his concluding remarks, he defended Eastern religion with great zeal. He predicted it would be helpful to Russia's future and was necessary to bring about a "beneficial connection of man with nature." Eastern religion and politics will eventually join together, he predicted, and lead people onwards and upwards toward an era of great hope.

What I encountered at the Institute for Science and Atheism in Russia is not an uncommon phenomenon. Some of evolution's top promoters in North America hold similar views. Although they refuse to acknowledge the God of the Bible, they have no difficulty in expressing the idea that everything is God or that God is in everything (panentheism). They are enthusiastically worshipping the creation rather than the Creator.

Another one of my early morning coffee shop witnessing experiences occurred several years ago when an elderly gentleman named Bob and I were discussing an article in the morning paper. I had expressed my ideas based on a Christian view. Bob was immediately outraged and asked if I was a preacher. I told him, no, I was not a preacher but that I did lecture on topics related to the Bible. He immediately broke out into hysterical laughter. Everyone in the whole restaurant looked around to see what was going on.

"What religion do *you* believe in?" I asked.

"I'm an atheist," Bob boasted. "I gave up that religious stuff a long time ago after I grew up and left home and was able to think for myself." He went on to describe how his parents had forced him to go to a Baptist church when he was a child.

"An atheist?" I quickly replied. "You're an atheist? This is exciting! I've never had the opportunity to meet one before. Do you mind if I ask you a question? What does an atheist believe?"

Bob responded by telling an off-color joke about a well-known Christian television personality, but he did not answer my question. When I continued to push for a reply, he finally said, "I am very close to Mother Nature. If you really want to know what makes the world tick, just look at Mother Nature. She'll tell ya." He then went on to explain about the hours he spent out in the woods and his garden, being "close to nature."

"Oh, Bob!" I responded when he had finished expounding on his view. "I'm disappointed. You're not really an atheist after all. You're a pantheist."

"What do you mean, a pantheist?" he asked. "What's that?"

"A pantheist is someone who rejects God as Creator but worships nature instead. It's someone like yourself who believes that nature is God."

"Okay, then I am a pantheist," Bob snapped. Then he went on to give more reasons why he had rejected Christianity when he was a small boy. From what he said, I deduced that he had once had a close encounter with Jesus Christ. Afterward, some experience that he refused to discuss had caused him to reject Christianity.

There are hundreds of thousands of people like Bob. Some say they are agnostics rather than atheists. They believe in something supernatural, but they do not know exactly what it is. Others simply avoid the question altogether, distancing themselves from God for reasons of their own.

God created every human being with a conscience and the ability to know right from wrong. Even if individuals deny that they believe in God, deep down inside they know their rebellious state of mind is wrong. Christians need to realize that no man or woman who has chosen to deny God is at peace. It is our responsibility to remind unbelievers of their need for God.

My conversation with Bob ended when I reminded him that one day he will have to stand before God. At that time, all the excuses in the world will not be sufficient. On several occasions since, we have had some interesting discussions about the Bible. My prayer is that someday Bob will come to understand the truth.

ARGUMENT NUMBER THREE: CHRISTIANITY IS TOO NARROW

One of the biggest criticisms of Christianity, especially now that we are in the "New Age," is that Christianity is far too narrow. The idea that there is only one way to God, and that Jesus Christ is that only way, is unacceptable to many people.

Of course, it is necessary to be tolerant and respectful of people who hold different beliefs. But respect for another's point of view is quite different from agreeing that other religions have valid methods of pleasing God.

Christianity is unique in that people are saved by accepting what God did; people of other religions must work to save themselves. Satan has convinced the masses there is something we must do to earn salvation. As a result, rituals, rites, and religious techniques are abundant. There are many ways to God in the eyes of the unbeliever. As the last days continue to unfold, the numbers of people being deceived will multiply.

Nick, a sixteen-year-old boy I met once in St. Petersburg, Russia, believed this way. He had been encouraged to come to an evening evangelistic meeting by a group of Americans who were street witnessing. He had been attracted by a drama presentation they were doing. As he stood and watched, one of the team members invited him to an evening meeting where I was speaking.

Nick was a member of the "White Brotherhood," a popular cult in Russia at the time. He was certain that he had already found God. The "God" he had found was the leader of his cult. Nevertheless, he agreed to come to the meeting.

That night, I was presenting a biblical perspective of the New Age movement. My purpose was to help explain Satan's strategy to deceive mankind, and I used the Bible to do so. After the meeting, a number of Christians tried to explain to Nick that he was on the wrong path. After almost an hour of trying to deal with his opposition, a person who was attempting to speak to him came over and asked me if I would talk to Nick and answer his questions.

It did not take long to realize that Nick did not have any questions, only answers. He was convinced that he was right and that the Bible was wrong. He thought he was on the road that leads to eternal bliss with God. He showed me several pictures of his cult leader, a lady who had told her followers she was God.

During our conversation, he indicated to me that he also believed Jesus was God. But so were Hare Krishna, Buddha, and several other gurus, including his own. "There are many ways to God," he said, "not just Jesus Christ. Your idea is too narrow."

After confirming that he believed in Jesus, I asked him a question. "Are you willing to listen to what the Jesus of the Bible said about what you believe?" He responded with a nod. I turned to Matthew 24 and read him verses 4 and 5:

> Take heed that no man deceive you. For many shall come in my name, saying, I am Christ; and shall deceive many.

He listened intently as my translator, Olga, read the words from her Bible in Russian.

Then we read two more verses from Matthew 24, verses 23 and 24:

> Then if any man shall say unto you, Lo, here is Christ, or there; believe it not. For there shall arise false Christs, and false prophets, and shall shew great signs and wonders; insomuch that, if it were possible, they shall deceive the very elect.

As soon as the translator had completed the two verses, Nick blurted out, "Well, I'm trying to live a good life. What's wrong with that?"

"That's a noble goal," I replied, "but the Bible verses I just read to you say that you are deceived. It is impossible to be perfect and without sin. Only Jesus accomplished that."

Nick and the friend with him shrugged their shoulders and walked away. However, they came back the next three nights. Members of our group continued to talk to them and to demonstrate Christian love as they shared their faith in Christ.

The last night in St. Petersburg at the end of the meeting, I asked if anyone wanted to ask for forgiveness of their sins and to invite Jesus Christ to come into their lives. As I finished the prayer, I glanced down from the platform, and there was Nick standing with his friend. Together, they prayed, acknowledging their sinfulness and need for a Savior, and asked the Lord to come into their lives. What an incredible miracle had taken place in just a few days.

Our group made sure Nick was put in contact with Christian believers in St. Petersburg. His new life in Christ had begun. The final night in St. Petersburg, as we were boarding the train to leave for Moscow, Nick and his friend showed up to see us off. As the train pulled away he waved joyfully. I will always remember the smile on Nick's face. Each time I think of him, I remember God's incredible grace.

ARGUMENT NUMBER FOUR: THE BIBLE IS A BOOK OF MYTHS

Christians are often criticized for taking the Bible too literally. Numerous derogatory phrases such as "narrow-minded militant fundamentalist" and "Bible thumper" have been coined to describe Bible believers. From day one, Satan's greatest objective has always been to get man to doubt and ridicule God's Word. He is still very successful at fulfilling that particular agenda.

Over the past several decades, one of the greatest threats to Christianity and to the authenticity of God's Word has been the doubts which Christianity has brought upon Christianity. Many seminaries and universities once committed to supporting the Bible, now seem dedicated to its demise. The Bible, modern scholars have said, is not relevant to the world today. It is an interesting book, but it must be upgraded for today's standards. Some suggest that the Bible is simply a mytho-poetic text, and that it is not written to be an authority on such subjects as science and origins.

The Bible is no longer respected as God's holy and inspired Word, contradicting what Paul stated that "All scripture is given by inspiration of God" (2 Timothy 3:16). Instead, it is viewed as an ordinary book which provides interesting reading, poetic verse, and spiritual ideas. Shall we believe in the inspiration of God or the inspiration of man? If the Bible is only partially true, which parts are true, and which parts are myth?

For a Christian to counter the criticisms of the intellectuals who have abandoned God, it is helpful to have a few facts at hand. If you are going to insist that God's Word and God's world agree, you need to come up with some reasons why you believe this to be so.

Most skeptics of the Bible have come to their conclusions through theories put forward by human reasoning not based on fact but rather on a secular variation of "faith." A study of facts drawn from biology, geology, and archaeology shows that what we know to be true about the world around us is not in contradiction with the Bible. Neither does a study of secular history and biblical history reveal contradictions when the facts are considered. What the Bible states about physical things is true. And what the Bible states about spiritual things is true as well.

Perhaps the greatest experiment that tested the truth of the Bible took place in the last century. The experiment did not take place in a test tube or a laboratory; it took place in a part of the planet that covers eleven time zones.

For over seventy years, the gurus of Marxist ideology in the former Soviet Union attempted to stamp out a belief in God. Bibles were banned. People who believed in the Bible were physically persecuted, imprisoned, and even killed. The effort was unsuccessful. How incredible it was to see what the God of the Bible did in the former Soviet Union after the collapse of communism there. The Gospel was proclaimed as a witness, just as Jesus said it would. Even the Russian Department of Education began encouraging the teaching of the Bible in an attempt to present morals and ethics which were ignored for so long.

The Bible is God's Word. It is true about the past, it gives understanding about the present, and it gives insights into the future. The Psalmist said it so well, "Thy word is a lamp unto my feet, and a light unto my path" (Psalms 119:105).

ARGUMENT NUMBER FIVE: SCIENCE HAS THE ANSWERS

Not only has the Bible been attacked by theologians, it has been brutally ridiculed by those who believe that science is the arbitrator of all truth. How can anyone question the authority of science? Much to the surprise of some, science does not have all the answers. On the subject of origins, for example, there is plenty of room for debate.

Another one of my coffee shop discussions took place with a non-believer named Ralph. "Science and scientific discussions," Ralph stated emphatically, "should be left to those in the field of science. Religion and religious beliefs should be left to those who espouse religion. It's foolishness to mix science and religion."

"I don't understand what you are getting at, Ralph," I responded. Please make yourself more clear."

"Well, you know, Christians are always trying to explain everything based on their interpretation of the Bible. They have a one-track mind. They have to line up everything they see with the Bible."

"But, Ralph, what do you think a Christian is supposed to do?" I asked. "Just because a fact agrees with the Bible doesn't make the fact religious. It's my view that the facts and the Bible already agree. You don't have to twist the evidence."

"What facts agree with the Bible?" Ralph asked. His choice to attack the Bible that particular morning couldn't have come at a better time. In the very paper I was reading, the *Orange County Register,* there was a photograph of a fossilized whale that had been unearthed just a few miles away. I opened the page and showed it to Ralph.

"Yeh," he grunted, "I already read the article. So what does that prove?"

"Well, give me your explanation of how the whale became a fossil, and then I'll tell you," I said.

Ralph offered a typical explanation derived from evolutionary dogma, describing how the whale had probably died a natural death and had been buried gradually over a long period of time and fossilized. After millions of years it had been uncovered for us to see today.

"Okay, Ralph," I interjected, "let me give you my explanation. Today, when a whale or any other animal dies, it decays. Am I right? Why didn't that whale decay? In fact, why do we have fossils? Why didn't life in the past rot like it rots today?"

I went on to present Ralph with an explanation of how fossils and layers of the earth were formed in a global catastrophic event, described in the Bible as Noah's flood. I even added a few more examples found in the fossil record to show how impossible it was for fossils to be formed in any other way except through sudden catastrophe. The Bible explains the fossil evidence much better than evolution. You do not have to be a fool to believe in the Bible.

Many people have lost their faith in the Bible because they have trusted in science. Their childhood beliefs have been swept away by the reasonings of man. Paul's warning to Timothy is for all of us:

> O Timothy, keep that which is committed to thy trust, avoiding profane and vain babblings, and oppositions of science falsely so called: Which some professing have erred concerning the faith."
> (1 Timothy 6:20-21)

ARGUMENT NUMBER SIX: I HAVE DONE A LOT OF GOOD THINGS

Some people resist the Gospel because they have convinced themselves they do not need God for salvation. When someone suggests to such a person that he or she is a sinner, their response will often be, "But I'm not a bad person. I have never stolen anything. I have never killed anyone. Basically, I am just a clean-living, law-abiding person."

Unfortunately, in the eyes of a holy, perfect, almighty, all-seeing, all-hearing God, good is not good enough. God does not keep a count of our good deeds and weigh them against our bad deeds on some cosmic scale. Even if He did, the Bible says that one single sin would be enough to tip the scale to a guilty verdict. Sin is lethal. Breaking God's law has a very serious penalty. "[T]he wages of sin is death" (Romans 6:23).

Sin is not only reflected by our actions. It also penetrates our thoughts. Jesus said:

> But I say unto you, That whosoever looketh on a woman to lust after her hath committed adultery with her already in his heart. (Matthew 5:28)

We are sinners, not only because of what we do and say, but because of the way we think. Is there anyone who can say, I have never sinned? The Bible answers the question for us, "If we say that we have no sin, we deceive ourselves, and the truth is not in us" (1 John 1:8).

When we compare our righteousness with God's righteousness, we come up short. As the Psalmist wrote and Paul quoted:

> There is none righteous, no, not one: There is none that understandeth, there is none that seeketh after God. They are all gone out of the way, they are together become unprofitable; there is none that doeth good, no, not one. (Romans 3:10-12; see also Psalms 14:1-3; 53:1-3)

Countless millions all over the world have come to Jesus Christ in repentance and faith after recognizing that a holy, righteous God will forgive them and give them eternal life if they will surrender their lives to Him and put their trust in Him for salvation. Paul stated:

> For by grace are ye saved through faith; and
> that not of yourselves: it is the gift of God:
> Not of works, lest any man should boast.
> (Ephesians 2:8-9)

These words that Paul proclaimed reflect my own testimony. After recognizing I had been deceived by evolution, I became a creationist, and then a Christian. The process from creationist to Christian occurred when I realized how imperfect I was in relation to God. No matter how hard I tried to live a life-style that would be pleasing to God, I could quickly see that I would always fall short.

In desperation one evening, I cried out in my own living room, "Oh God! Why do you even allow me to live? If you are perfect and I am not, and you can't possibly accept me unless I am perfect, why do you even allow me to live?"

Without actually hearing anything, a gentle answer was inscribed in my mind. *If you have come to believe in God as Creator, then you must also recognize Him as your Savior. The birth, the death, and the resurrection of Jesus Christ really did occur.*

I went to the Bible that my parents had given me on my ninth birthday and opened it to the very first page. There, in my father's handwriting, was a verse. As I read it out loud, my new life in Christ began: "For God so loved the world, that he gave his only begotten Son, that whosoever believeth in him should not perish, but have everlasting life" (John 3:16). From that moment on, I was changed forever. Thank God for His saving grace. He truly is our Redeemer.

ARGUMENT NUMBER SEVEN: GOD IS UNJUST

One of the questions unbelievers often ask regards human suffering. If there is a loving God who has created man, then why is the world so filled with pain, sorrow, fear, sickness, misery, and unhappiness? Why are there wars, famines, racial strife, ethnic cleansing, and other atrocities against humanity? Is God really in control? Is He a schizophrenic God? How can He say He loves us when He allows us to suffer?

The Bible can answer these questions and explain these circumstances with simplicity. The world in which we presently live is not the world God intended it to be. Once created in a perfect condition, it has been drastically affected by human sins, which are the consequence of Adam and Eve's choice to disobey the Creator. Since then, the earth has been subjected to a curse which has been passed down through the generations.

God created man with a free will, and man had a choice to know good and evil. When man chose to open the door to evil and disobey the Creator, suffering, misery, unrighteousness, wickedness, greed, malice, murder, strife, and envy were the consequences. Fallen people who are insolent, arrogant, boastful, without understanding, untrustworthy, unmerciful, unloving, and evil are not followers of God. They have turned their backs on God.

But the question remains, why does God allow it? If God can create a universe, can He not control the universe He created? History reveals times and places where evil forces wiped out whole segments of society from the scene. Is Satan and his evil realm more powerful than God?

The answer is clearly no. Satan is limited by God's authority, but man has the right to choose whom he will serve. If he chooses not to serve God, he becomes a servant of Satan. There is no middle ground.

Man is in his present predicament because of his free will. The opportunity to experience redemption from sin and to have peace with God is also a choice. But for the time being, God's original plan for man cannot be restored until Jesus Christ returns to bring the kingdom of God to the earth as it was originally intended.

For a student of the Bible, the world's present misery and lawlessness should come as no surprise. As Paul so clearly outlined:

> This know also, that in the last days perilous times shall come. For men shall be lovers of their own selves, covetous, boasters, proud, blasphemers, disobedient to parents, unthankful, unholy, Without natural affection, trucebreakers, false accusers, incontinent, fierce, despisers of those that are good, Traitors, heady, highminded, lovers of pleasures more than lovers of God. (2 Timothy 3:1-4)

Does that sound like today's world? Yet, despite the fallen society in which we live, God is still on the throne. Even though there are difficult times and circumstances, God has promised to work out His plan and will for our lives. As Paul so aptly said:

> [H]e that searcheth the hearts knoweth what is the mind of the Spirit, because he maketh intercession for the saints according to the will of God. And we know that all things work together for good to them that love God, to them who are the called according to his purpose. (Romans 8:27-28)

Until the Lord returns, the earth will not become a better place to live. It will only get worse and worse. But what a blessed future and hope for the believer, to be totally separated from Satan's domain. As John said in his Revelation vision:

> And I heard a great voice out of heaven saying, Behold, the tabernacle of God is with men, and he will dwell with them, and they shall be his people, and God himself shall be with them, and be their God. And God shall wipe away all tears from their eyes; and there shall be no more death, neither sorrow, nor crying, neither shall there be any more pain: for the former things are passed away. (Revelation 21:3-4)

ARGUMENT NUMBER EIGHT: CHRISTIANS ARE HYPOCRITES

One of the compelling arguments against Christianity is the behavior of certain Christians and the extra-biblical teachings many of them have adopted. These have provided non-believers with a smorgasbord of excuses for their rejection of the Gospel. They ask questions such as, "Why are there so many denominations? Which is the right one? How do we know if any of them are right?"

It is true that proclaiming Christians have separated themselves into a variety of groupings, ranging from Christians who are extremely legalistic, judgmental, and condemning to Word of Faith, New Apostolic Christians known for their spiritual gymnastics and high focus on signs and wonders, many of which are false and deceptive. The body of Christ is a multi-faceted organism. There are Christians who have the appearance of goodness and holiness but who are actually covering up secret destructive sins. In general, the broad spectrum of Christian behavior and belief often confuses the skeptic who is on the outside looking in on Christianity.

Another favorite excuse of the unbeliever who resists the Gospel involves the peculiar behavior of Christians and Christian leaders, especially those who have fallen from an elevated pedestal erected by adulating followers. The embarrassment suffered by the rest of Christianity because of these leaders continues to provoke jokes and laughter among the unchurched.

How do we continue to proclaim the Gospel despite these criticisms of the faith? Should we make excuses or deny the evidence? Should we protect ourselves from the cynical comments and attacks or face the music with some kind of defense?

Satan's greatest objective is to make Christians ineffective, and he knows that strange and unscriptural practices will always give Christianity a black eye. But the fact is this: all the foolish, sinful practices of a Christian can never keep the best-living non-believer out of Hell. Pointing fingers at others and calling Christians hypocrites cannot justify anyone of sin. Christians and non-Christians are both sinners. The difference is simply that one group is forgiven because they accepted God's gift of salvation and put their trust in Christ while the other has rejected that gift of being forgiven and saved.

Yes, it is embarrassing when a brother or sister brings shame and disgrace on the name of Jesus. But all Christians retain the free will to walk in the flesh. And this is where we stumble because if we live in the Spirit, we are also to walk in the Spirit (Galatians 5:25). Rather than point fingers and boast of our own righteousness, we need to remember that it is God's grace that keeps us, and any righteousness in us is a "gift of righteousness" (Romans 5:18) from God; thus, we cannot boast in ourselves but rather in what He has done for and in us. What great hope there is in knowing that even the greatest sinners can be made righteous in Christ if they will simply accept His offer of grace and forgiveness!

So, our answer to an unbeliever should be that Christians who stumble or walk in the hypocrisy of self-righteousness do not disprove Christianity but rather serve as a testament of God's patience with those who stumble and of everyone's need of the grace that can both save us and keep us through our Redeemer.

ARGUMENT NUMBER NINE: MAN IS SELF-SUFFICIENT

See if the following statement sounds familiar: "Christianity is a faith for the weak and the insecure." Or how about, "I am really happy for you that you have found religion. That's nice for you, and I wish you the very best. As for me, at least right now, I'm OK." Perhaps you have confronted these very words when you have tried to witness to someone.

The "I'm OK, you're OK" syndrome is a common strategy used to resist Christianity. Proclaiming one's own stability and security in the god of self is a defense mechanism commonly used by those rebelling against God. How can a Christian, and especially a new believer, confront people who proclaim such great self-confidence in human strength?

Of course, the goal of humanism has always been to spread the "gospel" of self-assurance as a means of attaining unfulfilled human potential. Man himself, without God, has long insisted that he is capable of directing human affairs, beginning with his own. The idea of a God who wants to save us by providing salvation and forgiveness of our sins seems to restrict man and is viewed as detrimental to the development of society. This is the perspective of those who place their trust in the humanist evolutionary agenda.

Although these humanists claim that the world is under the total control of mortal beings, the strongest followers of this philosophy will admit they have considered the possibility of a spiritual realm. Perhaps their brand of spirituality has carried them far away from the God of the Bible, but as they draw closer to the end of their life span, the question of the hereafter stares them in the face. The idea of reincarnation is not especially appealing when one is unsure as to just what form their next incarnation will take.

Why would anyone logically reject the free and certain gift of salvation and turn his or her back on God? Why would anyone want to spend eternity separated from Him? Who in his right mind would ever take the chance? Why not consider the possibility that there is a door that leads to Heaven? What has one lost, even if the choice is wrong?

Deep down, no matter how successful or secure he or she may seem to be, every thinking person has doubts and fears about life after death. Some honest, pointed questions from a genuine sincere believer can often jolt the skeptic into reality.

ARGUMENT NUMBER TEN: TODAY'S WORLD OFFERS A NEW SPIRITUALITY

In our so-called postmodern progressive society, millions of people around the world are being deceived by the greatest lie that has ever been told. The path to self-esteem, self-realization, and godhood is being blindly traveled by countless individuals who, in actual fact, are on their way to Hell. To further complicate matters, the Bible and certain supposed teachings of Jesus are being offered as proof that the "New Age" is the way and the truth for the unsuspecting.

Shortly after moving from Canada to southern California, I met Carol, a young lady who was showing me an apartment. During our conversation, Carol asked me why I was moving to California. I told her I was a lecturer, and that the topics I spoke about included the creation-evolution controversy and the "New Age" movement.

The moment I said "New Age," Carol's eyes lit up. "Oh, I am very interested in that subject," she said. "I would love to hear what you have to say about it."

"Well, that's possible," I said. "I'll be speaking on that topic Monday night at Calvary Chapel. Why don't you come?"

"Oh, Monday night isn't a good time for me," she said. "Monday night, my husband and I have our weekly appointment with our guru."

For a moment, I was at a loss for words. "Your guru? You're going to see a guru?" I almost choked for lack of words.

Carol further explained the situation. Although she had been brought up in a Catholic home, she had fallen away from the faith because of her disillusionment with the church. After marrying her husband who had come from a Presbyterian background, the couple had jointly decided that life must have more of a spiritual emphasis than either had experienced in their youth. One day, they came across a brochure advertising a seminar about techniques that would bring peace and happiness by looking "within oneself" through meditation and Yoga.

After listening to Carol's story for a while, I finally interrupted. "So what has been your experience?" I asked. "Have you found the peace that you were looking for?"

"I think so," she stammered. Her tone of voice belied her words. Recognizing that God had placed me there for this moment, I asked if she would mind hearing my perspective from the Bible about what she was involved in and what she needed to do to find real peace.

I told her she could find the peace she was searching for if she simply asked God to forgive her for her sins and accept the gift of eternal life that the God of the Bible has provided.

Carol, like so many others who have rejected Christianity for one reason or another, are part of a large group of people who have never heard the Gospel presented clearly and understandably. They yearn for spiritual reality, but they are searching in the wrong places. And, of course, Satan, like a roaring lion, is all too happy to lead them down the road to eternal deception.

"Higher consciousness" is the goal of Eastern religions. Associated with it are techniques and therapies, from ancient to the modern, all promising the self-deification of men and women. Meditation, Yoga, chanting, breathing techniques, crystals, hallucinogenic drugs, hypnosis, and many other methods all lead to the same destination. Unfortunately, that destination is not the God of the Bible. Sadly, many proclaiming Christians today have become involved in various eastern-style meditation practices such as breath prayers, centering prayer, lectio divina, and contemplative prayer. And an increasing number of evangelical churches are now holding Yoga classes for their congregants.

The idea that God is a force or an energy that permeates all things and that creation is all a continuum of God is not a biblical idea. The God of the Bible is separate from creation (Romans 1:25), and He must be worshipped as the One who made all things (Revelation 4:11). God is not a force that flows through all things and can be manipulated or harnessed. The claim of Eastern philosophy that man can be God or can find God by "looking within" is a total delusion. God is not *in* anyone with the exception that the Holy Spirit indwells those who have accepted Jesus Christ as their Savior—who promises to be their comforter and guide.

Furthermore, the lie that the human race is living at the time of a "great awakening" and that joining the religions of the world will bring about peace and prosperity to the planet is another lie. A continued journey down the road of mysticism and the occult will bring nothing short of God's hand of wrath and judgment and what the Bible refers to as "strong delusion," not a great awakening.

Those who have committed their lives to Jesus Christ have always faced opposition from the satanic realm. To be confronted by a resurgence of paganism before the return of Christ should come as no surprise. It is our privilege and responsibility as believers to share the Good News with this generation as well as to give God's perspective of the "New Age" and where it will ultimately end.

MANY MORE EXCUSES

Of course, these ten arguments are not the only ones you will ever face. It is encouraging to know that whatever the challenge, God has not left us in the dark. Jesus Himself wanted His followers to be salt and light to the world. It will encourage you if you will keep these words in mind when you are confronted with disagreements and debates about the Gospel:

> Ye are the salt of the earth: but if the salt have lost his savour, wherewith shall it be salted? it is thenceforth good for nothing, but to be cast out, and to be trodden under foot of men. Ye are the light of the world. A city that is set on an hill cannot be hid. Neither do men light a candle, and put it under a bushel, but on a candlestick; and it giveth light unto all that are in the house. Let your light so shine before men, that they may see your good works, and glorify your Father which is in heaven. (Matthew 5:13-16)

—9—

ARE YOU READY?

U p until now, this book has discussed ideas, ways, and means that can be used for witnessing. But now we are about to consider the most important principle of all: putting words into action. If you only remember one lesson from this book, it would be my desire that you would remember that being a witness for the Lord Jesus Christ in this generation is as simple as one, two, three:

- You must be available for God to use you.

- You must be sensitive to God as He leads you.

- You must do what you said you would do.

It is worth repeating that no one comes into the kingdom of God through human effort alone. Soul winning is a partnership between God and man. Although God is not limited by man's involvement, for some reason He often chooses man to be a part of the process of leading one to the foot of the Cross. Because of this, sensitivity to His leading is a key factor when it comes to witnessing.

How easy it is to establish our own human schedules and to proceed with our own plans. But without the guidance and direction of the Holy Spirit, human effort, intelligent reasoning, and clever manipulation simply are a waste of time. Prayer is the best way to determine God's will for our lives, and every believer has been given the privilege of having a personal "hot line" to God. It is essential that we consult Him in every situation and specifically when it comes to sharing the Gospel.

It is also apparent from the Scriptures that the most important prerequisite for being used by God is a willing servant's attitude. Throughout biblical history, the numbers of people willing to serve have never been significantly large. God has always looked for a few servants who are completely sold out to Him. As the Bible states in 2 Chronicles 16:9:

> For the eyes of the LORD run to and fro throughout the whole earth, to shew himself strong in the behalf of them whose heart is perfect toward him.

WHEN WE FIRST BELIEVED

Born-again believers like to recall the excitement and enthusiasm they experienced when they first met the Lord. Perhaps for some it was a casual experience. However, for most Christians, the initial meeting with the Lord was one of exuberance and unlimited joy. What greater experience could you ever anticipate than welcoming the Creator of the universe into your very own heart? In those early days, what a desire each one of us had to tell others about Him. We wanted them to experience with us the incredible gift of eternal life, accompanied by a peace that passes all understanding.

This initial enthusiasm to tell others can be an accurate indication that a person has truly become a Christian believer. Family members and friends are soon exposed to the new-found truth offered by the convert as he or she zealously proclaims that Jesus Christ has made a difference in his or her life and that the Bible truly is the Word of God. In some cases, waves of conversions follow, as one new believer begins to share with others.

However, quite often that new-found enthusiasm for Christianity disappears after a while. Other things interfere. The love relationship with the Lord dwindles. The exhilaration gradually fades away. The path from a promoter to a supporter to an indifferent observer of the Gospel is too commonly traveled by Christians. And certainly Satan does not leave new believers unattended. Making new Christians ineffective is part of his strategy to make sure the lost have little opportunity to hear about God.

God has a life purpose for every believer. The question is, what have we done to fulfill our call? Not everyone is called to be a great evangelist, gifted to reach the masses. Nor can all of us proclaim the truth from a pulpit, or write books, or have a program on radio or television. But each of us has a part, however small it may seem, as a participant in God's overall plan to reach the lost. In God's economy, it is not important how many you have reached; the important thing is that you reach those you have been called to reach.

1. ARE YOU AVAILABLE?

Availability is the first qualifying factor for Christian witnessing. God will not force you to be His servant. It must be your willful choice.

David, the shepherd boy, was one of the greatest witnesses for God in the history of mankind. When Samuel was asked by the Lord to go to the family of Jesse to choose a new king for Israel, God gave these instructions:

> Look not on his countenance, or on the height
> of his stature; because I have refused him: for the
> LORD seeth not as man seeth; for man looketh on
> the outward appearance, but the LORD looketh
> on the heart. (1 Samuel 16:7)

God observes each human heart, seeking genuine commitment and total trust. David had these qualities. And that is why, although David was an unlikely candidate in man's eyes, God chose him for the elevated position of king. Not only was David willing to be God's servant, but he also was a man of great courage, relying totally upon God. When confronting the mighty Philistine warrior Goliath, David boldly said:

> [W]ho is this uncircumcised Philistine, that
> he should defy the armies of the living God?
> (1 Samuel 17:26)

In later years, the prophet Nathan communicated a message from God to David, saying:

> I took thee from the sheepcote, from following the sheep, to be ruler over my people, over Israel: And I was with thee whithersoever thou wentest, and have cut off all thine enemies out of thy sight, and have made thee a great name, like unto the name of the great men that are in the earth. (2 Samuel 7:8-9)

The prerequisite for being used by God is not special credentials that have been earned by human effort, but commitment and availability. God's plans have no boundaries. And to encourage us even further, Jesus chose these words when He said to His disciples, "Follow me, and I will make you fishers of men" (Matthew 4:19). These same words, spoken to His disciples, are for you and me today. If we are willing to follow Him, He will do the work of making us effective witnesses.

2. ARE YOU LISTENING?

The Bible teaches that the God who created the universe and everything in it has a timetable for each day of our lives. According to Psalm 139, He not only knows what we are doing, He knows what we are going to do before we do it. Recognizing that God has a plan for each and every day, our greatest desire as Christians should be to live our lives in accordance with His will.

This tiny glimpse of a sovereign God makes it clear that no individual crosses our path by pure chance. Each day of our lives is full of experiences that have been set before us. These opportunities allow us to demonstrate to others our belief in the Gospel, either through our actions or through our words.

It is very important to listen when God speaks to us in the course of our daily lives. The Bible is filled with examples of the way God communicates to individuals as to where, to whom, and how they should witness. A very interesting account is recorded in the book of Acts, chapter 8.

Following the stoning death of Stephen, a number of the followers of Jesus Christ left Jerusalem. They spread themselves around the country proclaiming the Gospel. Philip went down to Samaria and proclaimed Christ to the people there.

The Bible records that Philip's ministry in Samaria was a great success:

> And the people with one accord gave heed unto those things which Philip spake, hearing and seeing the miracles which he did. For unclean spirits, crying with loud voice, came out of many that were possessed with them: and many taken with palsies, and that were lame, were healed. And there was great joy in that city. (Acts 8:6-8)

Considering the exciting account about the effectiveness of Philip's ministry in Samaria, and the large numbers he was reaching, we might assume he had been called there for long-term work. But God's plan for Philip took a sudden turn. An angel of the Lord supernaturally spoke to Philip and told him to "Arise, and go toward the south unto the way that goeth down from Jerusalem unto Gaza, which is desert" (Acts 8:26).

Philip obeyed, and as he was travelling this secluded road in a very desolate area, he came upon an Ethiopian eunuch who was a court official of Candace, the queen of the Ethiopians. The eunuch had traveled to Jerusalem to worship and was on his way home. Philip noticed he was sitting beside his chariot, reading a portion of the Scriptures from the prophet Isaiah. The Bible then tells us, "Then the Spirit said unto Philip, Go near, and join thyself to this chariot" (Acts 8:29).

Philip approached the eunuch and engaged him in a conversation. The conversation centered around the verses the eunuch was reading and a question he had in his mind about the verses he had read. Philip answered his question by using the Scriptures from Isaiah, and as the Bible states, Philip "preached unto him Jesus" (Acts 8:35).

Shortly thereafter, as they were traveling down the road together, the eunuch said, "See, here is water; what doth hinder me to be baptized?" Philip responded by saying, "If thou believest with all thine heart, thou mayest." The eunuch answered by saying, "I believe that Jesus Christ is the Son of God" (Acts 8:36-37).

This account provides us with some wonderful lessons about witnessing. First, God's plan to reach the lost is not limited to large numbers of people, but it also includes one-on-one conversations. As illustrated in Philip's case, the same person can be used to do both. It is not the number of people converted by a particular person that matters; it is the obedience to God's call that makes the difference.

God may choose to speak to us in several different ways. His method of communicating to us may be supernatural, or it may be quite ordinary and mundane. But one thing is sure, when God speaks, there is little doubt.

It is encouraging to remember that when God asks us to be His spokesperson, He has often already prepared the hearts of those He has asked us to reach. Romans 1:19-20 tells us that God reveals Himself to unbelievers. And it is the work of the Holy Spirit to draw them to Christ. As with Philip and the eunuch, our circumstances may well be the clue for us that we have been called to speak personally to a certain person in a particular place.

3. ARE YOU READY TO FOLLOW?

It is essential that we understand the grace of God if we are to become soul winners. God is an all-knowing, all-powerful, almighty and without a flaw God. Man is limited in understanding, weak, unstable, and extremely inadequate on his own. The grace of God makes us realize how big God is in comparison with very small men and women.

However, it is important to realize that God delights in using weak and inadequate people who are willing to depend upon Him. That way, when God's plan unfolds, no one individual can take the credit and the glory. As Paul stated, every servant of God should acknowledge the source of his ability and say, "I can do all things through Christ which strengtheneth me" (Philippians 4:13).

This "Christ-in-us" principle is the number one key for true success, no matter what we are trying to accomplish. Following His guidance each moment of each day is the second most important factor.

Not being sensitive to God's direction can often get us into difficult territory. Human beings are inclined to work out their plans and agendas according to their own ideas. Endorsing the "if I do this" then "God has to do that," theology causes untold problems.

For example, people frequently approach me after a seminar, asking me to recommend a book or tape that might help convert some unsaved relative or friend. I usually say something like, "One of my books might be useful in planting some seeds, but there are certainly no guarantees."

"But my dad is a scientist who believes in evolution," they will say, or "My cousin is heavily involved in the New Age. I just know that the information you presented in your seminar would show them they are wrong."

At that point, it is my responsibility to remind them that the battle they are facing is spiritual, not intellectual. God may use the information contained in a book or a tape, but the best thing to do is pray. Start with prayer, and if God leads you to do something more, respond accordingly.

Every day of our Christian lives should be a day completely given over to the Lord so His plan and purpose for us can be worked out. To be in harmony with Him, it is vital that we stay in daily communion with Him; we can do that through the reading of His Word and by prayer. When we commit ourselves to being available servants for the Lord, the opportunities He will provide for us will be unlimited. I know this is true. He has done more with my life than I could have ever imagined possible.

A TRANSFORMED LIFE

As a child, before being formally educated, I had no reason to doubt the existence of God. However, through my final years of high-school education and later as I spent a number of years at university, the idea of God as a Creator was gradually replaced by the theory of evolution. As intellectual arguments replaced common sense, and as humanistic reasoning replaced logic, I gradually became another zealous promoter of the evolutionary theory.

For several years, I taught biology from an evolutionary perspective. Then a major change took place in my life. My father suddenly passed away, forcing me to make a decision. Would I continue in the teaching profession, or would I return to the rural community where I grew up and manage our family farm?

Throughout the years that I was at the University of Saskatchewan, both as a student and a teacher, I had abandoned the Christian values and beliefs of my youth. Although I had everything one could want materially to be happy and successful, my life was empty and filled with frustration. In short, I was self-centered, unhappy, and hopelessly lost.

It was at this point that God began to miraculously show His hand. Beginning with the loss of a child, my wife Myrna and I found that our lives were drastically changing. Information flooded to my attention which completely altered my worldview. Gradually, I recognized that what I had believed about evolution was a great delusion. After changing from an evolutionist to a creationist, I finally became a born-again Christian.

Almost immediately, I started to research and gather information which supported the biblical Christian view. I became part of a seminar team, speaking at churches and conferences throughout western Canada, sharing the evidence that supported the Bible and the reality of Jesus Christ.

Ten years after becoming a Christian, when I reached the age of forty, I prayed a prayer which profoundly changed the direction of my life: God, make me willing to be willing to do what you want me to do.

It was my sincere desire to make the rest of my life count for eternity. From the moment I prayed that prayer, I can say without any exaggeration, my life has truly been a great adventure.

In 1988, I was invited to become part of the staff of Calvary Chapel of Costa Mesa, in California. My wife and I could see that God's plan was being unveiled through circumstances beyond our control. So we responded to the call that we believed was upon our lives and left our relatives, friends, and farm in Saskatchewan, Canada and made the move to Southern California.

During my years at Calvary Chapel, doors for ministry opened throughout the United States, as well as in various international venues. God led us to form a missionary organization called Understand The Times, which has given us the opportunity to speak and share the truth of the Bible in over fifty countries.

Without a doubt, the greatest miracle we witnessed was the door that opened to the former Soviet Union. There, where people were once persecuted for believing in the Bible, God opened the door for "creation evangelism" in a most incredible way. I had the opportunity to travel to Russia and other countries on dozens of occasions. Conferences, lectures, and meetings were held with scientists, teachers, professors, pastors, and Department of Education officials. Two of my books and three videos were translated into Russian and were widely distributed.

I share this to underscore the fact that the God of grace and mercy is in the business of changing lives. All that has been accomplished in your life or mine, past, present, or future, is a testimony of God's grace. It has nothing to do with *our* goodness or ability. Success in God's work is a gift from God.

Our Creator wants to use every available, willing candidate. He wants to use me. He wants to use you. The question that each one of us must ask ourselves is: are we willing and available to do what we actually say we are willing to do? Think of the tremendous things God can accomplish through our lives if we are completely willing and available to serve Him.

—10—

THE LANGUAGE OF LOVE

What kind of people make the best witnesses? The kinds of individuals God uses as messengers of the Gospel vary greatly. There are no set patterns, no ideal examples that must be followed. As unique and different as the members of the family of God are, so are the gifts and the opportunities that God assigns to each individual.

Our willingness to witness clearly reflects the relationship between ourselves and God. A loving relationship with God on the vertical plane will strongly influence how we are able to relate to men, women, boys, and girls on the horizontal level. It is impossible to have a strong desire to reach out to others if we are only concerned with ourselves. Being wholly self-focused is the direct opposite of having a godly nature. We must do everything we can to turn our attention away from ourselves and turn it to God. Then we will be concerned about others.

People who seek to promote evangelistic programs sometimes attempt to develop rules or guidelines for witnessing.

These ideas can be useful; however, with God we need to remain open and flexible. Witnessing should be voluntary, not forced or manipulated. Sharing the Gospel should be exciting and joyful, not a chore.

Communicating the message of salvation should be a life-style, reflected steadily in our lives. It should be the life-long vocation of every Christian—from the moment of our new birth in Christ to the day we pass on to be with Him for eternity.

AN ADDED INCENTIVE

What is this life all about? Why are we here? Where are we headed in the future? For a Christian, these ought to be easy questions to answer. God created man to have a relationship with Him. Man has been given the choice to reject God or to live in harmony with Him for ever and ever.

Regarding the certainty of our man-made plans, the Bible stresses caution. James commented:

> Go to now, ye that say, To day or to morrow we will go into such a city, and continue there a year, and buy and sell, and get gain: Whereas ye know not what shall be on the morrow. For what is your life? It is even a vapour, that appeareth for a little time, and then vanisheth away." (James 4:13-14)

When compared to eternity, our lives really are nothing more than a moment of time. Every heartbeat and every breath we take is a valuable gift from God. Of course, we should be wise enough to consider our mortal nature. And it makes perfect sense for us to do everything in our power to make sure we are in harmony with our Creator.

But, as I have already noted, the obstacles to faith and obedience are numerous. Like everyone else, many believers become consumed with the pressures of everyday life. Goals and objectives of a spiritual nature, which were initially important to us, can easily get placed on the bottom shelf.

Maybe it is time we reassessed our priorities. Stop for a moment and think about some of your acquaintances. Perhaps it's your mother, your father, a daughter, or a son. Maybe it's a friend, or a neighbor, or perhaps an employee at work. Or it could be a person you met on vacation, a student going to university, or an elderly person in the hospital. You may have thought briefly about these people and their spiritual destination, but the thought slipped away.

Has God been speaking to you about sharing His message of salvation with them? Have you heard His voice in the midst of your busy schedule? Or have you thought that there are others who would be more adequately prepared and equipped to deal with an unbeliever's excuses not to believe?

What has God's Spirit been saying to you?

The "rules" in the game of life are quite simple. Whoever dies rejecting God's offer of salvation spends a lost eternity separated from God. But whoever believes in Jesus will not perish but will live with Him forever. There are no alternatives and no second chances. Every moment that goes by brings each person one moment closer to his or her ultimate encounter with death.

Time is running out for all of us. The time until Jesus returns appears to be very short. This should serve as an added incentive for us to work faithfully among our lost friends and loved ones.

THE NATURAL MAN

Sometimes we become frustrated with the unbelievers in our lives, asking ourselves "why don't they just see the light and believe? Why is it so hard for them to understand? Why can't they just accept the truth? It's so simple!" Many frustrated Christians share these sentiments. But to the unredeemed, the need for Jesus is a major blind spot.

To understand the position of a person who does not have the spirit of God dwelling within them, it is helpful to read what Paul told the Corinthian believers. He wrote:

> Now we have received, not the spirit of the world, but the spirit which is of God; that we might know the things that are freely given to us of God. Which things also we speak, not in the words which man's wisdom teacheth, but which the Holy Ghost teacheth; comparing spiritual things with spiritual. But the natural man receiveth not the things of the Spirit of God: for they are foolishness unto him: neither can he know them, because they are spiritually discerned. (1 Corinthians 2:12-14)

When in rebellion against God, men and women always attempt to reason the God of the Bible out of existence. By their own foolishness, they will reject God's wisdom and replace it with their own. There are two ways of approaching these people. One is relational, and the other is confrontational.

RELATIONAL WITNESSING

Relational witnessing is a day-in, day-out process. It means demonstrating Christianity by our actions. In my own estimation, it is the foundational basis for all other methods of witnessing. A casual survey of new believers will reveal some very interesting statistics. The numbers of individuals introduced to Christ by someone who first befriended them far exceed those who converted through another method of evangelism.

Perhaps a Christian drew close to them at a time of need, during a family tragedy or a crisis situation. Or it may have been a friend at school who offered an invitation to go to church or a concert. There are many ways to express concern and caring. But there is no substitute for taking the time and the effort to put someone else ahead of our selfish interests.

To a person who is searching, love expressed by an action may well say more than a thousand words of human wisdom. As Jesus explained:

> A new commandment I give unto you, That ye love one another; as I have loved you, that ye also love one another. By this shall all men know that ye are my disciples, if ye have love one to another. (John 13:34-35)

By demonstrating concern, listening, praying, providing necessary help, and by living a consistent godly life for others to see, the ground is often prepared in the hearts of unsaved friends or relatives before the actual seed of the Gospel is planted. As we have seen again and again, both the preparation of the soil and planting of the seed are important to the salvation process. But, as always, ultimately it is God who brings forth life and growth.

CONFRONTATIONAL WITNESSING

Relational witnessing is essential but, unless further steps are taken, the non-Christian remains unchallenged about making a decision to accept Jesus Christ. Many people observe some Christian's lifestyle and admire it. But they do not have a clue as to what they need to do about living the same way. Confrontational witnessing is simply a means to communicate the message of salvation loud and clear.

Presenting the truth of God accurately can take a variety of forms. Less personal means include providing written tracts, books, audio tapes, video tapes, or even suggesting that the person be exposed to something on radio, television, or film. The seeds of truth planted by these various methods are often successful in winning skeptics to Christ. Other popular methods include the preaching of the Gospel from the pulpit in evangelistic sermons and mass crusades. People who bring friends or relatives to these kinds of meetings have a special role to play. They are part of the evangelistic team.

One of the most effective ways to be a confrontational witness is to challenge a person head on in a conversation. When the time comes, and you are certain the Lord is leading you to speak, then speak. If you have spent time getting to know the person and are aware of his or her needs and sensitive to the issues involved, you should be well prepared. Now, when God leads, your most reliable way of presenting the Gospel will be to communicate in your own words, face-to-face, heart-to-heart, the wonderful gift of salvation Jesus has to offer.

UNCONVENTIONAL WITNESSES

Sometimes, confrontational witnessing goes to peculiar extremes. Some evangelistic enthusiasts may actually do more harm than good in their attempt to share the Gospel.

Every Christian has had the experience of being embarrassed by unrealistic, overzealous promoters of the Gospel. One cannot help but question the effectiveness of some of these methods.

One year when I was attending the Expo event in Vancouver, British Columbia, I was approaching the exit gate of the grounds one summer afternoon when I noticed a strange-looking man handing out tracts. He was dressed in a long, thermal winter overcoat and wore a conspicuous sign around his neck that read: "Sweating for Jesus." There was little doubt that he was sweating. The temperature that day was over 100 degrees Fahrenheit. Less obvious was any success he may have been having as a witness.

In the same city several years earlier, while I was a speaker at a seminar, an elderly lady enthusiastically shared with me her method of street witnessing. She claimed she had "won" many people to the Lord. Then she explained to me her method: "I hide in the bushes beside a sidewalk early in the morning," she chirped. "When people come by, I just jump out and shout,

'Get saved, or you'll go to Hell!' It's amazing how this frightens people," she added.

Unconventional styles of witnessing may work, if God is at work in them (or in spite of them). But experience seems to reveal that, by far, their success is the exception rather than the rule.

THE MIDDLE OF THE ROAD APPROACH

Usually the best approach to anything is a balance between two extremes. Although there are times and places when either relational, confrontational or unconventional witnessing fits the situation, usually a combination of the first two is the best compromise.

The key to witnessing is being sensitive to God's leading and prompting by His Holy Spirit. Although very few of us may ever hear God's voice audibly, His instructions come clearly and in various forms. Being ready and willing in all circumstances is the best preparation for being used as a communicator for the Lord. Establishing relationships and expressing the gentleness, humility, and love of the Lord often opens the door to a golden opportunity to directly proclaim His love. Sometimes these opportunities take years to present themselves; in other cases, they may come along after only a few minutes have passed.

A WITNESSING TEAM

While I was in the process of writing the first edition of this book, I had an opportunity to witness God's Spirit in action right before my own eyes. A group from a Christian

Bible college traveled with me to St. Petersburg and Moscow for a two-week tour. The objective of the trip was to share Christ with people in a country that had not heard the Gospel for a very long time.

The team was made up of various personalities, all of whom had different gifts, characteristics, and abilities to serve the Lord. Some passed out tracts, some spoke publicly, some ministered in song. Others used puppets, performed skits, played musical instruments, and even played football with the children. The Gospel was communicated in a number of ways, and everyone had a part to play. Through all of this, I discovered some very important principles about witnessing: *God is faithful. He does the work; and He gets the job done His way.*

The last night we spent in Moscow was a memorable occasion. We had hosted a very interesting meeting, during which several cult members had generated some opposition. Afterward, several of our team gathered at a Pizza Hut, along with a translator by the name of Yuri. Yuri was a 34-year-old nuclear scientist with a doctorate degree. He told us he was an atheist and that he had been coming to the church in Moscow because he wanted to practice his English.

While we were seated around the table eating pizza and enjoying our time together, we asked Yuri to tell us about himself. We were all curious about his point of view. It was apparent that he was disillusioned with life, desperately empty, and without peace. After listening to him for a while, all four of us seated at the table shared our personal testimonies with him.

Dan, one of our team, explained how he had become a Christian after attending an evangelical church and was impressed by the love of God that he saw in the people. Stephanie described how God had been her strength through her battle with cancer and how her life was now completely devoted to her Savior. Tom told how his attitude as a businessman had been revolutionized by an encounter with Christ. I related how God had changed me from a cynical agnostic to a true believer and how I now had the desire to share the reality of Jesus with others.

Over the course of the evening, something unusual happened. During this trip, we had been challenging people to accept Christ, often in a confrontational way. Yet not one of us felt led to ask Yuri if he wanted to pray and accept Jesus Christ as his Lord and Savior. Instead, we simply watched his countenance change as the evening progressed. His stoic, stern face showed signs of relaxing. Eventually, he smiled. As he guided us back to our Moscow dormitory, he started to laugh and join in our light-heartedness. Something was happening to Yuri. A transformation was beginning to take place.

The following day, I was ready to depart. The others were staying one more day. We gathered together for prayer. Before I left, I asked Stephanie, who was going to stay for an extra week, to make sure she spent some more time with Yuri.

Just about a week later, a wonderful message came to me from Moscow. Stephanie's report confirmed that God's miraculous hand of grace had been with us the night we had spent time with Yuri. As I had surmised, we had experienced the soil being prepared and the seed being planted. God Himself had brought forth the miracle of new spiritual life. Yuri was now a member of the family of God.

NOW IT'S UP TO YOU

There is nothing more vitally important than the Gospel and what it means for anyone who by faith accepts it, believing on the work that Jesus Christ did on the Cross to pay for our sins. What each person does with it will determine where he or she will spend eternity.

Although there are many Christians sincerely dedicated to doing their part in proclaiming the Good News, there are others who sit on the sidelines and do not participate. It is my prayer that everyone who reads this book will be encouraged to take their part in the proclamation of the Gospel message to this generation.

Why not take a moment right now and ask God to help you for this purpose? Perhaps you could pray a prayer that goes something like this: Heavenly Father, I pray that you would make me willing to be a witness for you. I desire to serve you, and I want to be available for whatever it is that you would want me to do. Help me to be sensitive to your Holy Spirit as you lead and direct me in the way you want me to go. I will place my hand in yours and follow you.

EPILOGUE

I charge thee therefore before God, and the Lord Jesus Christ, who shall judge the quick and the dead at his appearing and his kingdom; Preach the word; be instant in season, out of season; reprove, rebuke, exhort with all longsuffering and doctrine. For the time will come when they will not endure sound doctrine; but after their own lusts shall they heap to themselves teachers, having itching ears; And they shall turn away their ears from the truth, and shall be turned unto fables. But watch thou in all things, endure afflictions, do the work of an evangelist, make full proof of thy ministry. (2 Timothy 4:1–5)

ENDNOTES

Chapter 4: Messengers on a Mission

1. *Los Angeles Times*, A3, March 4, 1992.
2. Ibid.
3. Ibid.

Chapter 5: Creation Evangelism

1. For a compelling 14-lecture series on creation vs. evolution, watch Roger's DVD set *Searching for the Truth on Origins.* Available through Lighthouse Trails.

Chapter 6: Evolution: Physical or Spiritual?

1. Jean Houston, *The Possible Human,* Introduction, p. 17.
2. Dr. Brian O'Leary, *Exploring Inner And Outer Space, A Scientist's Perspective On Personal and Planetary Transformation,* (Berkeley, CA: North Atlantic Books, paperback edition, 1989), p. 42.

ABOUT THE AUTHOR

Roger Oakland is an author, lecturer, and the founder of Understand the Times, International. He has written several books and is featured in numerous documentary DVD films. Over the past 35 years, he has lectured in over 70 countries. His autobiography *Let There Be Light* chronicles his years as an evolutionist to becoming a creationist and then a believer in Jesus Christ. In a new updated edition published in 2011, Roger shares the intimate story of his son, Bryce's death at the age of 27, which eventually led to the founding of the Bryce Homes Program, a missions program that ministers to the physical and spiritual needs of Christian widows and children in several different countries.

You may contact Roger at:
Understand The Times
P.O. Box 27239
Santa Ana, CA 92799 USA

Understand The Times
P.O. Box 1160
Eston, Saskatchewan, Canada SOL 1AO

Visit Roger's website at http://www.understandthetimes.org.
Also visit www.lighthousetrails.com for more of Roger's materials.

BRYCE HOMES
INTERNATIONAL

Serving the needs of
Christian widows and orphans
around the world.
www.understandthetimes.org

BRYCE HOMES PROGRAM FOR WIDOWS AND CHILDREN

Bryce Homes International was founded by Understand The Times in 2002 as a program to assist Christian widows and orphans around the world. The program is in memory of Bryce Oakland, son of Bryce Homes founder Roger Oakland and his wife Myrna, who passed away in 2002.

The program has expanded over the years to include Myanmar, Kenya, the Philippines, South Africa, Haiti, Mexico, the USA, and India. Presently, there are over 500 children in 80 homes.

Through donations, Bryce Homes International is able to provide housing, monthly food support, education, latrines, clothing, and certain medical needs to these families. In addition, Bryce Homes is developing a pilot program in Kenya in which Bryce widows are able to begin their own cottage business that gives them the means to sustain themselves so that they may become self-sufficient, allowing other widows to enter the program.

While Bryce Homes International helps to meet the physical and educational needs of these widows and children, their spiritual needs are also addressed. The children as well as the widows are taught the Word of God and are encouraged in their personal walks with the Lord by local pastors who have been mentored by Bryce Homes International.

OTHER RESOURCES BY ROGER OAKLAND

BOOKS

Another Jesus: The Eucharistic Christ and the New Evangelization ($12.95)

Faith Undone: The Emerging Church—A New Reformation or an End-Time Deception ($14.95)

Let There Be Light (Roger Oakland's biography) ($14.95)

The Evolution Conspiracy: The Impact of Darwinism on the World and the Church (with Caryl Matrisciana) ($14,95)

The Good Shepherd Calls: An Urgent Message to the Last-Days Church ($14.95)

DVDs

The Emerging Church Lecture series: Man's Spiritual Journey, the Road to Rome, the Road to Babylon, Proclaiming the Gospel

Searching for the Truth on Origins Lecture Series

The Wiles of the Devil Lecture: End Times Deception in the World and the Church

BOOKLETS ($1.95 each)

A Christian Perspective on the Environment

The New Missiology: Doing Missions Without the Gospel

The Catholic Mary and the Eucharistic Christ

The Jesuit Agenda

The New Evangelization From Rome or Finding the True Jesus Christ

Atonement Rejected!

How to Know When the Emerging Church is Showing Signs of Emerging Into Your Church

The Reformation: A Brief But Important Look

Rick Warren's Dangerous Ecumenical Path to Rome

Roger's materials are available through Lighthouse Trails. You can also visit www.rogeroakland.com and www.understandthetimes.org to access articles Roger has written. Several of Roger's materials are also available in Spanish.

OTHER BOOKS FROM
LIGHTHOUSE TRAILS PUBLISHING

A Time of Departing
by Ray Yungen, $14.95

Chains Couldn't Hold Me
by Cedric Fisher, $14.95

Changed by Beholding
by Harry Ironside, $11.95

Father ten Boom, God's Man
by Corrie ten Boom, $13.95

For Many Shall Come in My Name
by Ray Yungen, $13.95

Foxe's Book of Martyrs
by John Foxe, $14.95, illustrated

How to Prepare for Hard Times and Persecution by Maria Kneas, $14.95

How to Protect Your Child From the New Age & Spiritual Deception
by Berit Kjos, $14.95

In My Father's House
by Corrie ten Boom, $13.95

Muddy Waters
by Nanci des Gerlaise, $13.95

Out of India
by Caryl Matrisciana, $14.95

Seducers Among Our Children
by Patrick Crough, $14.95

Simple Answers: Understanding the Catholic Faith by Ray Yungen, $12.95

Stories from Indian Wigwams and Northern Campfires
by Egerton Ryerson Young, $15.95

Strength for Tough Times, 2nd ed.
by Maria Kneas, $11.95

Taizé—A Community and Worship: Ecumenical Reconciliation or an Interfaith Delusion? by Chris Lawson, $10.95

The Color of Pain
by Gregory Reid, $10.95

The Trinity: The Triune Nature of God by Mike Oppenheimer, $11.95

Things We Couldn't Say
by Diet Eman, $14.95, photos

The Gospel in Bonds
by Georgi Vins, $13.95

The Other Side of the River
by Kevin Reeves, $12.95

Trapped in Hitler's Hell
by Anita Dittman, $13.95

For a complete listing of all our books, DVDs, and CDs, go to www.lighthousetrails.com, or request a copy of our catalog.

To order additional copies of:
Witness to This Generation
Send $12.95 plus shipping to:

Lighthouse Trails Publishing
P.O. Box 908
Eureka, Montana 59917

For shipping costs:
($3.50/1 book; $5.20/2-3 books; $10.20/4-20 books)
You may also purchase Lighthouse Trails books from
www.lighthousetrails.com. The bulk (wholesale) rate for10
or more copies is 40% off the retail price. For U.S. & Canada
orders, call our toll-free number: 866/876-3910.
For international and all other calls: 406-889-3610
Fax: 406-889-3633

Witness to This Generation, as well as other books by Lighthouse
Trails Publishing, can be ordered through most major outlet stores,
bookstores, online bookstores, and Christian bookstores in the U.S.
Bookstores and libraries may order through: Ingram, SpringArbor, or
directly through Lighthouse Trails.

For more information, visit our research site:
Lighthouse Trails Research Project
www.lighthousetrailsresearch.com

Lighthouse Trails has a free weekly e-newsletter and a bi-
monthly subscription-based 32-page print journal. Visit www.
lighthousetrailsresearch.com, or call one of the numbers above to
sign up for the free e-newsletter or to subscribe to the print journal.
($15/year for U.S. | $29/year for CA | $42/year for international).

Made in the USA
San Bernardino, CA
19 January 2019